IMAGES
of America

ESCONDIDO
GRAPE DAY FESTIVALS

The Mexican survey that created Rancho Rincon del Diablo was conducted on horseback, relying on natural formations to pinpoint the boundaries. The three square leagues included the best land in the valley. Markers were often obliterated, making land claims disputable. An American survey of the rancho, carried out with more accurate methods, officially registered 12,653,77 acres in 1858. Lewis Ryan's 1968 drawing illustrates the differences. (Courtesy PR.)

ON THE COVER: Movie star Agnes Ayres, crowned queen of the 1923 Grape Day Festival by Maj. Gen. Joseph H. Pendleton (left) faces her adoring Southern California subjects at the 16th annual celebration. Never before had a queen of the silver screen reigned over the event. She rode to the park on a horse-drawn float surrounded by heralds, pages, wood nymphs, and butterflies. Ayres performed with Paramount and Famous Players-Lasky. (Courtesy EHC.)

IMAGES
of America

ESCONDIDO
GRAPE DAY FESTIVALS

Lucy Jones Berk
and Stephen A. Covey

ARCADIA
PUBLISHING

Published by Arcadia Publishing
Charleston SC, Chicago IL, Portsmouth NH, San Francisco CA

Library of Congress Control Number: 2008922713

For all general information contact Arcadia Publishing at:
Telephone 843-853-2070
Fax 843-853-0044
E-mail sales@arcadiapublishing.com
For customer service and orders:
Toll-Free 1-888-313-2665

Visit us on the Internet at www.arcadiapublishing.com

Grape Day 2007 dawned with yet another royal party proceeding down the traditional parade route, Grand Avenue to Grape Day Park. From a 1914 Overland touring car, Grape Day queen and king, author Lucy Jones Berk and husband William E. "Bill" Fark, welcome the crowd. The author decrees eternal gratitude on Bill for encouraging, cooking, laundering, and keeping the wine glass full during her years of research. (Courtesy NCT.)

CONTENTS

ACKNOWLEDGMENTS

Making their version of Eden, Escondido pioneers layered over 100 years of history in the valley before the Sunkist Vale became my home. A sign facing Broadway identifies a downtown oasis as Grape Day Park. This unusual name sparked my journey to learn why a grape would be so celebrated. Many wonderful people shared memories and materials on Grape Days past, adding variety and flavor to the project.

At Escondido History Center, director Wendy Barker, Robin Fox, Shirley Buskirk, and Richard Bartley; and at Escondido Public Library Pioneer Room, archivist Helene Idels, Nancy Salisbury, and Ruth Collings pointed out obscure files, photographs, and facts.

Heartfelt gratitude goes to Stephen A. Covey, a true partner who not only scanned photographs but provided every technical need except turning on my computer; Frances Beven Ryan, pioneer descendant, recorder of her Grape Day experiences, and harvester of much of the materials available on the Escondido festival; Ellen Sweet for guidance; Evie Berk for excelling; and my editor, Debbie Seracini, whose patience outlasted the vicissitudes of my life.

Special thanks for access to memory, written, and photographic collections to Margaret Armstrong; the Escondido Chamber of Commerce; the Oceanside, San Marcos, and Valley Center Historical Societies; Judith A. Downie at California State University San Marcos Library; June Osborne, Aspen Hill, Jack Owens, Christine O'Connor, EHC past director Norman Syler, Katherine Barber Fromm, Leone O'Neal, Joseph Swoboda, Edith Swaim of Oceanside Heritage Park, Mardell Ehmke Theiler, Katherine Rombaur Thornton (KRT), Wisdom/Warnes Archive (WWA), and Hugh Young.

Detailed descriptions of Grape Days appear in the *San Diego Union*, *Los Angeles Times*, and *Escondido Daily Times Advocate*. At the latter, now the *North County Times* (NCT), managing editor Rusty Harris authorized use of a contemporary photograph and columnist Jeff Frank spread the word for helpful sources.

Unless otherwise noted, most of the photographs came from two archives, Escondido History Center (EHC) and Escondido Public Library Pioneer Room (PR).

My glass of liquid grapes is raised in tribute to all who assisted in the fruitful harvest!

INTRODUCTION

The Grape Day festival, first taking place in Escondido in 1908, was preceded by discovery, settlement, and development of the fertile but arid inland valley. Indigenous peoples gathered acorns and springwater for eons. Spanish explorers and missionaries skirted the area, establishing a chain of missions at which the native people would be converted to Christianity while providing a free labor force. During the Mexican-Californio period, Mexican government officials carved out the 12,653-acre Rancho Rincon del Diablo land grant for faithful citizen Juan Bautista Alvarado. *Rincon del Diablo* means Devil's corner in Spanish and is said to indicate that this land was never a holding of the missions, in contrast to church-owned ranch lands located to the west and south, whose grant names all begin with *san*, such as San Marcos and San Bernardo. Jose Maria Orosco, Alvarado's son-in-law through marriage to daughter Guadalupe, inherited a portion of Rancho Rincon del Diablo. The earliest discovered use of the name Escondido appears on a mortgage document securing a $350 debt between Orosco and William H. Moon dated November 1852. Orosco refers to his property as Ranch of Escondido.

Over time, Oliver S. Witherby, U.S. Border Commission member, bought the entire grant from Alvarado's heirs for less than $4,000. This purchase began a new era, bringing the land into Yankee hands. Witherby specialized in entertaining, raising cattle, and prospecting for gold. In 1868, he sold the ranch to the Wolfskill brothers and Edward McGeary, who raised sheep on the newly named Wolfskill Plains. The little settlement that occurred was mainly in the northern end of the valley. Speculators from Stockton, incorporated as the Escondido Company in 1884, purchased the property, at $10 an acre, for the production of wine grapes on the plain along the north side of Escondido Creek. A state agronomist had declared the soil and climate in this valley the most conducive to the growth of grapes he had ever seen. The partners planted 100 acres in muscat grape cuttings imported from Europe and named the area the Big Vineyard. Unprecedented rains damaged the crop, discouraged the partners, and, in 1886, prepared the way for a new investment group that envisioned a town site surrounded by large farms and ranch lands.

The Escondido Land and Town Company (EL&TC) purchased Rancho Rincon del Diablo for $104,042. Collectively, the dozen men who formed the corporation were well versed in the various skills necessary to develop real estate into a community. Composed of transplants to San Diego, the group included four Thomas brothers from Kansas. For 10 years, the little town grew steadily until a severe drought and a five-year national depression took their toll. Families left; businesses closed, and the bank nearly failed. The water problem had to be resolved. A system was conceived by the Escondido Irrigation District to bring water through flumes from the San Luis Rey River to a reservoir at the east end of town. Voters approved bonds to cover the cost, and the challenging project was completed, but at great expense. The financial strain of the water bonds on the community was overwhelming. Relief eventually came in 1905, when bondholder H. W. Putnam accepted 50¢ on the dollar in settlement to retire the $228,000 debt. Heated discussion followed as to the best way to dispose of the cancelled paper. Many felt a commemorative event should mark this accomplishment. Merchant Sigmund (Sig) Steiner suggested a public burning of the bonds. The plan grabbed the imagination of civic leaders and citizens alike as a time for solemn festivity. Regional dignitaries and Southland residents were invited to share the happiness. Admission Day, September 9, was the date chosen, as it was a statewide holiday honoring California's joining the Union in 1850. Enthusiastic visitors flooded into town. Under a banner proclaiming "FREEDOM," a procession headed up Grand Avenue from the depot to the historic conflagration of the bonds on the steps of the grammar school. The burning remained in the local memory.

On subsequent Admission Days, families gathered on the tree-shaded school grounds to picnic, socialize, and pay homage to Bond Burning Day. In 1908, Mayor Sig Steiner suggested that a commemorative celebration be held annually on that date, September 9. Prominent businessman W. L. Ramey was mulling over a similar thought: a promotional event to introduce newcomers to the unique features of Escondido. He had recently attended a booster festival in Anaheim. "Freedom" from debt morphed into "Free Grapes" for all visitors who would invest a day in experiencing the wonders of the Hidden Valley. The planners agreed that honoring the valley's major crop, the bountiful grape, by offering free samples to all comers and carriage tours of the vineyards, town, and valley, would spread the good word about the Sunkist Vale. The celebration would be called Grape Day and always be held on September 9, except when it fell on a Sunday. All residents of San Diego County were invited to enjoy Escondido's abundant and luscious grape crop: "All the grapes you want to eat, right off the vines. Free as the air." A special six-car train from San Diego was arranged. So many visitors joined the 1,500 townsfolk that the population doubled for the day. A resounding success, and seen as a positive promotional tool for the city, Grape Day took hold. City fathers established a board to guide the festival, and every aspect grew grander each year. Several regional celebrations around the state became extremely popular, including Fresno's Raisin Festival, Santa Cruz's Water Carnival, Stockton's Old California Day, and Riverside's Orange Day. But for many years, only the Tournament of Roses Parade at Pasadena attracted more visitors than Grape Day. These two festivals proved the longest lasting in the state. Developments in newspaper publishing and photography made a big impact on all the promotions, including Grape Day.

Louis Havens moved to Escondido in 1911, becoming the first professional photographer to make a living at the craft locally. By recording Escondido events, development, and people, Havens captured the community for posterity and for distribution around the country through newspapers, magazines, and chamber of commerce brochures. The previously merged weekly *Times-Advocate* newspaper achieved new ownership in 1912, when purchased by Percy Evans and Ernest N. White. Within a month, they turned the property into a daily publication, proof of their confidence in the growth potential of the Escondido region. In time, the company would produce Grape Day Special Editions, prized by collectors today. Festival offerings and crowds grew each Grape Day. The parade, displays, and entertainments grew annually, with the crowd finally reaching an estimated 40,000 people in 1947. When a star of the silver screen participated in the 1923 festival, a motion picture was filmed for distribution in theaters nationwide. Radio broadcasts shared features of the day over the airwaves. Local girls and visitors posed in vineyards for pictures that drew attention to the Sunkist Vale. By the 1940s, pinup-girl photographs of Grape Day queen candidates, usually paired with luscious local grapes, become especially popular in publications and helped spread the good news about Escondido. The celebration of Escondido agriculture and progress continued through the Great Depression, took a hiatus during World War II, and resumed through 1950. Escondido remained the market center of the region as the agricultural laurel passed from vineyards to citrus and avocado groves. Three major packinghouses for citrus and one for avocados shipped fruit to markets and wineries across the country and for export. Many people in the valley worked as growers or packers, suppliers of agricultural equipment or in supporting businesses.

World War II and the cold war brought many changes, as military training camps and defense factories brought a surge of new residents to an inadequate housing stock. Both the community's focus and economy changed. Agricultural lands proved more valuable as housing developments;

science took precedence over old ways; diversity had arrived. People looked to the skies, not the ground. The dissolution of the Grape Day Association effectively ended a tradition. Leaders tried various fairs, carnivals, and festivals. Western horse clubs became popular after the war years, sponsoring parades and horse shows that commanded attention. A weak attempt at a Grape Day revival in 1959 drew only 5,000. The only celebration to take hold was the Junior Chamber of Commerce (Jaycees) Christmas parade, started in 1951 and still drawing crowds every December. When "old-timey" things became popular after the nation's bicentennial, the Escondido Historical Society decided to sponsor an annual harvest-themed fair in Grape Day Park. A legal issue required a name change for the event in 1996. The historic "Grape Day" was selected. Each September, Grape Day is commemorated with a parade, prizes, queen, entertainment, club displays, craft booths, food and, yes, free grapes, The current population of nearly 140,000 includes many transplanted residents with little knowledge of the valley's heritage and an overwhelming array of activities to occupy their leisure time. Percy Evans, former publisher of the *Times-Advocate*, reminisced in 1949: "Motion picture stars have cast their brilliant light on the crowd. . . . Nationally known characters have added their lure to the program. Political speakers have given their eloquence to the crowd at Grape Day Park, but the homecoming visits of the people . . . have been the spirit that makes Grape Day beloved." Evans refers to people now long gone. Grape Day, however, again grabs attention, promoting the area's agricultural past and sense of community into the 21st century.

A Cluster of Grapes grown in Escondido Valley, California.

Luscious green-colored muscat grapes grew profusely on bottomland in the congenial Escondido climate. This variety, giving the best average return, is hardy and thrifty, yielding especially large berries and heavy clusters. Because of the strong skin, the meaty fruit stays on the vine without deterioration and ships well for table use. The muscat also makes excellent raisins. Other varieties of table and wine grapes do well in the Hidden Valley. Escondido's deed restriction on alcoholic beverages did not prevent local wineries from producing thousands of barrels of juice for shipment to wineries in California and Mexico. During Prohibition, making homemade and sacramental wine was permitted. The repeal of the federal law opened the door for legal manufacturing of wine in Escondido. This relieved stress for numerous growers who had been previously accused of illegal production and distribution of table wines. (Courtesy EHC.)

One

ROOTSTOCK

Escondido Land and Town Company (EL&TC) grabbed the opportunity to purchase Rincon del Diablo for $5 an acre in 1886. The development company officers were Jacob Gruendike, Daniel P. Hale, Thomas E. Metcalf, and brothers Richard A., Charles E., John R., and William W. Thomas. From San Diego, the company promoted the valley, toured prospects about in a tallyho, and began construction of a 100-room hotel to host buyers. Quickly a bank, brickyard, and lumber company arose along dusty Grand Avenue. A local EL&TC office opened. Amasa Sibrent Lindsay agreed to publish a weekly newspaper, the *Escondido Times,* to spread word of the growing community throughout the Midwest and South, where like-minded settlers might be found. Graham and Steiner General Merchandise Store relocated from Bernardo. Settlers arrived to establish homes, businesses, and farms. Brick-lined wells tapped water for domestic use from beneath the creek bed. EL&TC succeeded in establishing a town that, within two years and with a population around 500, incorporated as a city in 1888. Growers planted more acres in grapes, and the bulk of these harvests went to the table or raisin trays, as the manufacture and sale of alcoholic beverages was prohibited by EL&TC deeds. A red brick seminary, affiliated with the University of Southern California, soon towered over the town from a hilltop. Seven churches, given lots by EL&TC, established congregations; six built edifices of Escondido-made bricks. The railroad came in 1888, induced by an offer of $110,000 from the Escondido and San Marcos land companies. Grapes, grain, and groves flourished, but most fruits did not ship well, and markets were far away from this hidden valley. Grapes, especially the muscat variety, proved to be excellent travelers, and were lauded as an enduring crop. Grapes and pioneers, within the unstable parameters of agriculture, enabled Escondido to grow and prosper, making a name and product known across the country and in foreign lands.

The Wolfskill brothers and Edward McGeary purchased Rancho Rincon del Diablo from O. S. Witherby in 1868 for the purpose of raising sheep. Thousands of acres of grassy valley land with natural creeks provided the animals all they needed to thrive. Wool proved a valuable commodity, and the partnership prospered. This first house in Wolfskill Plains was built in the 1870s. (Courtesy PR.)

A view of the expansive valley, looking west from the eastern edge, shows the Engelmann oak trees growing thick along Escondido Creek. *La huerta* (the orchard) was treasured by Native Americans, Californios, and Yankees alike. The Escondido settlement is 3 miles in the distance, with the Big Vineyard in between. (Courtesy PR.)

A 160 Acre Vineyard, Escondido, Cal.

This 160-acre vineyard (above) is the property of John C. Dickson, revered as Escondido's raisin king for the volume and quality of his sun-dried grapes. The exhibit he entered in the 1893 Chicago World's Fair won awards and brought honor to the valley. To make raisins, grapes bunches were put directly on redwood trays and left in the field to dry in the sun. The Thomas Show Ranch, later known as Eureka Ranch (below), exhibits the wide variety of fruit trees that would thrive in the Sun Kissed Vale. (Above, courtesy EHC; below, courtesy PR.)

Returning from the cemetery, townsfolk parade along Grand Avenue on Decoration Day 1894, honoring those fallen in the Civil War. Commercial buildings frame the north side of the street: from left to right, Escondido Times building, Cravath building, Escondido National Bank, New York store, and Moon's and Stevenson Brothers' two-story brick stores. (Courtesy PR.)

Percy S. Cox's 1894 photograph looking west from College Hill offers a view of the businesses (right) clustered along Grand Avenue. The residential area south of downtown shows a scattering of houses along Indiana and Iowa Avenues. The east-west streets were named after Midwestern states to entice prospects to buy on the street named for their state of origin. (Courtesy PR.)

14

The need to house prospective investors was urgent. Not waiting for completion of the brickyard, EL&TC ordered immediate construction of the three-story Escondido Hotel out of wood. The hotel, seen here around 1887, perched on a commanding knoll at the east end of Grand Avenue, becoming the community social center. The former landmark was demolished and recycled in 1925. (Courtesy PR.)

The first brick buildings rose at the northeast corner of Grand Avenue and Lime Street beginning in spring 1886. Escondido National Bank commanded the corner. EL&TC set up shop in a bay facing Lime Street. A one-story structure (left) housed the *Escondido Times*, first printed November 4 of that year. Thomas Cravath built the adjoining two-story building in 1887. (Courtesy PR.)

E. A. Merriam promoted his Globe Brand California Raisins with this gorgeous lithographed label that could serve as a poster and cover art on a confectionary box of the sun-dried fruit. The woman may be Demeter, Greek goddess of agriculture and fertility. She wears a gown of deep pink, gold-trimmed at the hem. A luscious bunch of muscat grapes rests at her feet. A gold-girdled cherub holds a box covered with the identical design while happily accepting a fresh bunch of fruit. Escondido is indicated in red on the California map. The foreground landscape resembles Hidden Valley vineyards and hills. Merriam's name, listed as a farmer, does not appear later than the 1901 local directory. (Courtesy © WWA.)

16

Two

WATER WOES TO BLESSING FLOWS

Promotion of Escondido's abundant sun, soil, and water lured enough settlers by 1889 to render the water system inadequate. The EL&TC system of pumping water from the creek to a small reservoir for gravity feed to customers could not keep up with demand. The Escondido Irrigation District was formed that year. An 1891 vote approved $350,000 in obligation bonds to pay the costs of diverting water from the San Luis Rey River, 25 miles east, by blasting mountain rock and constructing trestles over canyons to a large earthen-dam reservoir. The project, nearly insurmountable with hand tools, began in 1893 and required the labor of 400 men. As drought withered the crops, washouts and fires destroyed much of the undertaking, requiring continuous repairs. A nationwide recession brought havoc; many people abandoned stakes and moved on. Every settler felt the financial burden of the water bonds. The Escondido National Bank managed to survive but was the only one in the county to stay open. A deal was struck with H. W. Putnam to redeem the bonds at 50¢ to the dollar. Relief overwhelmed the citizens, and many offered suggestions for disposing of the virtually worthless bonds. Until a consensus could be reached, they were stored in the bank vault. Sig Steiner proposed a ceremonial burning and promoted the scheme by presenting his customers with a special "freedom" sale. The plan spread like wildfire, and a region-wide incineration was organized to express to the world the overwhelming relief from debt felt by the people of the Escondido valley. The city leaders chose Admission Day, a holiday, as the perfect time for the grand burning. Invitations went out to officials, organizations, and citizens throughout the county. Leaders made arrangements with the Santa Fe railway for special excursion rates from San Diego and Los Angeles. Escondido would mount the greatest celebration in its 19-year existence. The "Burning of the Bonds" took place on the steps of the Lime Street Elementary School on September 9, 1905.

The rugged, mountainous terrain through which the irrigation system workers persevered presented a challenge as well to regional photographer Percy S. Cox as he lugged bulky equipment to record the event for posterity. In this 1893 image (above), diggers who followed the blasters shovel out a ditch before lining it with wood. An 1895 photograph (below) shows the completed flume snaking along the hillside between the peak and the canyon below. Natural conditions bedeviled workers with scorching heat, poisonous snakes, insects, and the constant fear of falling. (Courtesy PR.)

E. I. Doty and Company was contracted to construct the system. J. D. Schyler engineered the flumes and ditches needed to transport the water to Bear Valley Reservoir. A photograph of Cape Horn illustrates the extreme terrain of the upper 4 miles, above the Rincon Indian Reservation, that the project had to surmount. (Courtesy PR.)

Crews filled the ravine at the west end of Bear Valley with blasted rock and earth. They completed the 80-foot dam in 1894. Water filled the lake by Christmas Eve 1895, doubling the joy that night. Householders and ranchers reveled in the improved supply of life-giving water. (Courtesy PR.)

The Hidden Vale looked rosy in 1905. With the water system completed, ditches and flumes repaired with concrete, and the burden of the water bonds lifted, people were in a celebratory mood. Escondido Mutual Water Company had taken over the old irrigation district. Growers shipped 13 tons of muscat grapes to Los Angeles during the first harvest week. Sig Steiner designed and distributed "Escondido is All Right: Burn the Bonds" buttons (left) to promote his plan to celebrate and savor the occasion. The chamber of commerce board accepted the advice of Mayor Steiner to hold the event on Admission Day. Steiner (below) ordered 600 baskets to hold grapes for the visitors. This was seen as the time to lure home seekers. (Courtesy PR.)

Graham and Steiner built an imposing brick store (above) in 1897. An auditorium, wired for the electricity to come, occupied the second floor, the first such public space in the city. Steiner, a new breed of merchant, offered specials and premiums to his customers. After Graham left, Steiner and Company promoted itself as "the people's store" and celebrated the grand incineration with a "Bond Burning–Freedom Day Sale in All Departments." The First National Bank (below) was completed in 1905 just in time for visitors' inspection as they strode on newly completed concrete sidewalks. Designed by San Diego architects Hebbard and Gill, the bank faces Grand Avenue, across Lime Street from the Steiner emporium. Many more improvements such as H. N. Lyon's Escondido Mercantile greeted visitors. (Courtesy PR.)

Fresh capital was pumped into agriculture as well as buildings. John J. Johnston Jr. purchased the Big Vineyard in 1903. His wife, Dell Hale Johnston, daughter of EL&TC partner Daniel Hale, shared ownership of the pioneer vineyard for many years. The Big Vineyard became known as the Johnston Vineyard, where unidentified men pose in this 1910 photograph. (Courtesy EHC.)

Properly preparing fruit for shipping long distances by railway was as vital to the industry as good growing practices. The Loveless Fruit Company, owned by Ellery and Robert Loveless, provided packing services in Escondido for nearly 20 years. Packinghouses employed many women, such as these boxing raisins for market in 1904. (Courtesy PR.)

Escondido Times dispatches to California newspapers and invitations to civic leaders, and organizations spread the word of the upcoming "funeral." Santa Fe railway provided special round-trip rates from San Diego ($2) and Los Angeles ($3). Every available buggy was recruited to transport female guests and dignitaries from the depot. Men and bands march alongside forming an impromptu parade (above) toward a banner spelling "FREEDOM" in grapevine letters above a large national flag. Tours were offered. Church and club ladies prepared and sold lunches to the guests. Following the touring and dining, 1,500 guests and 1,500 residents proceed up North Lime Street to the grammar school grounds (below) to enjoy the program and the burning of the bonds. (Courtesy PR.)

BOND-BURNING CELEBRATION
PROGRAM

Saturday, September 9th, 1905

[W. A. SICKLER, Chairman Program Committee]

1. Song—"Praise God, From Whom All Blessings Flow ".......................... By Audience
2. Instrumental Solo .... Miss Case
3. Music.................... San Diego City Guard Band
4. Vocal Solo......... .... Miss Annis
5. Male Quartette—Messrs. Thomas, Lawrence, Justice, and Hoover.
6. Vocal Solo...................... .... Miss Williams
7. Music............. .... City Guard Band
8. Duet.. ....Misses Williams and Annis
9. Speech..........................Hon. J. N. Turrentine
10.   BOND BURNING
By Old Directors of Escondido Irrigation District: Messrs. Larzalere, Bowen, and Blodgett.
11. Song—"America" ....Audience

ESCONDIDO TIMES, Pioneer Newspaper of Interior San Diego

No hymn better expressed the joy of the citizens than "Praise God from Whom All Blessings Flow." The committee arranged a program (left) of appropriate solemnity. Local talent and the San Diego band entertained. Venerable Judge J. N. Turrentine (center stage below) stirred the audience with eloquence: beginning his speech with "The borrower is a servant of the lender," and closing "Now let the bonds be burned." The bonds were ignited in a wire basket above the platform. Flames leaped, filling the air with smoke. Suddenly a rope controlling the cage's height burst into flame and the inferno crashed to the ground, mission completed. Visitors left with baskets of free grapes, and the local folk "possessed new life and fresh hope," commented *Escondido Times* editor A. S. Lindsay. (Courtesy PR.)

Three

CELEBRATING

THE HARVEST

Escondido gained confidence from the outstanding success of the bond burning celebration. When back home, every visitor spread the good word about the Hidden Valley. Newspapers and magazines up the entire West Coast and across the country ran articles on the accomplishments and promise of Escondido. The name *Escondido* would be known by the superior quality of its grapes, community, potential, and hospitality. Sig Steiner encouraged an annual commemoration, and W. L. Ramey agreed to chair a festival to honor the grape and promote the valley. An event was born: Grape Day, held on September 9, 1908, both Admission Day and the anniversary of the bond burning. Sig Steiner is esteemed as the "Father of Grape Day," although he was never board president. Festivals provided guests with parades, tours, entertainment, oration, and free grapes. Crowd estimates were strictly guesses, but locals were correct to appraise most years as bigger and better than the preceding. The festival grew in size and complexity: floats, queens, more bands, agricultural displays, visiting delegations, sports competitions, automobiles, and an occasional outstanding event. In 1912, a permanent Grape Day Board was formed to relieve the chamber of commerce, formerly in charge. At the suggestion of writer and artist Isaac Frazee, the city acquired the old school ground as a park, soon to be called Grape Day Park. The name Escondido was on many tongues, but the physical and financial demands stressed the community. During the early years, each production created a struggle, but not even World War I disrupted Grape Day. Directorship changed frequently until the late 1920s, but free grapes and hospitality were always available in Escondido on September 9.

Escondido families gather at the Lime Street School grounds to enjoy picnic meals with friends on Admission Day. In 1906 and 1907, the outing became an anniversary celebration of the burning of the bonds. While children played along the creek edge, adults reminisced with joy about that happy day and shared thoughts about the improving economy. (Courtesy PR.)

Ripe grapes are sun-dried to raisins at an Escondido vineyard around 1900. Growers contracted for migrating crews of pickers to harvest the grapes into redwood flats. Left in the open to dry, flats were rushed under shelter by a frantic gathering of local men and boys to prevent ruin of the harvest when a sudden rainstorm hit. (Courtesy PR.)

W. L. Raney served as president of the first Grape Day Festival. He came to Escondido with his friend A. W. Wohlford in 1892 to rescue the failing Escondido Bank. Ramey held great confidence in the valley's future and became a leading booster. He managed the Escondido Lumber Company and in 1910 built a commercial hotel that bore his name on Grand Avenue. Ramey and Steiner made a fine team in planning and promoting the first festival, aided by commerce secretary and newsman James H. Heath. The success of Steiner's bond-burning button led to the 1908 Grape Day button (below), a bunch of plump green muscat grapes on a field of purple. Another tradition was born. (Courtesy PR.)

SAN DIEGO
ESCONDIDO
EXCURSION

❀

GRAPE DAY

❀

SEPTEMBER 9,
1908

Newspaper advertisements promised "all the grapes you want to eat right off the vines, free as the air" at the Grape Day Festival. A special excursion train brought visitors from San Diego at reduced $1.50 round-trip rates and with distinctive ribbons (left) that made them stand out in the crowd. Members of the event committee, Ramey, Steiner, Bradbury, and Hedges, boarded the train at Oceanside for the ride to Escondido, handing out Grape Day buttons and free grapes to the guests. The depot presented a well-organized mob scene, with teams and buggies surrounding the "free grapes" wagon (below center) lined up to transport visitors on tours of the valley and to the festivities centered on Grand Avenue between Lime and Maple Streets. (Courtesy PR.)

Empty lots along Grand Avenue became center stage for displays and entertainment (above). Men covered a framework with boughs and palm fronds, which women and girls covered with grapes, vines, and leaves to create a giant, shady arbor. Agricultural products of all types grown in the region, especially an impressive variety of grapes, were displayed on tables. Churchwomen conducted a lunch counter, and barrels of free lemonade were available to refresh the guests. Uniformed marchers (below) pass beneath the grapevine banner defining the occasion at the main intersection. Nearby hung a large golden key with the slogan "Yours for Today." (Above, courtesy PR; below, courtesy EHC.)

Following the San Diego City Guard and Escondido Coronet bands, Knights of Pythias members, dignitaries, visitors, and citizens formed a parade led by Russell Cox on horseback (above). A 1908 Ford horseless carriage caused excitement. Bringing up the rear of the procession, a wagon (below) carries hundreds of pounds of free grapes for the sampling and enjoyment of the crowd. Merchants and residents decorated downtown buildings and homes with cheesecloth dyed green and purple in the grape theme and bunting of red, white, and blue to honor the state's birthday. Businessmen vied with each other for facade- and window-decorating kudos. (Courtesy EHC.)

There was more, or less, to the arrival of the excursion rain than expected. The number of celebrants required six railcars, a heavier train than had ever ventured inland from Oceanside. The train ground to a halt on San Marcos's Richland hill, requiring an unhitching and separation. The first segment arrived an hour late; the second arrived at 2:30 p.m., missing the parade. Mounted cowgirls (above) greet passengers with grape-decorated letters spelling "W-E-L-C-O-M-E." They whiled away the wait for the second section by transposing the letters to "L-E-M-O-N," jeering the railway company. The equestrians are, from left to right, Marie Witte, Iris Conner, Nellie Stiles, Lena Larzalere, Frankie Willard, and Zora and Gail Wisdom. Grape Day officials (below) gather with some of the 5,000 people who enjoyed Escondido's first Grape Day. (Above, courtesy PR; below, courtesy EHC.)

Stories of men in the air seemed words of fantasy at the end of the 19th century. To witness such an event stirred the hearts of all. A Professor Earlston created the entertainment excitement of the first Grape Day with the ascension of his hot air balloon from near the great grape arbor. The committee hired Earlston to rise above the crowd in his balloon while seated on a bicycle and descend by parachute drop. Suddenly the contraption rose with a rush. Earlston was unable to loosen the parachute. The crowd expected disaster, but professor, bicycle, and balloon settled gently on the roof of N. Butler's house a few blocks south, where Earlston jumped unhurt to the lawn. The crowd felt the thrills and chills of averted tragedy. Though weary, guests departed with happy memories and free grapes and basked in the success of their special day. (Courtesy EHC.)

Grape Day Festival 1909, under the guiding hand of merchant G. W. Wisdom, had competition. The county fair took place at Lockett's Rock Springs Farm, 2 miles from downtown, on the same day. The doubleheader, however, brought people interested in both events. Two special trains from San Diego delivered 1,800 people, and one from Los Angeles transported 500 more. Many former Escondido residents returned to see the progress. Two women of the Grape Day Committee (above) lead the procession back toward the Grape Arbor. The wagonload of grapes (below) nears its destination at the arbor in a photograph that shows the enormity of the temporary shade structure. (Courtesy EHC)

Grapes were in evidence everywhere in 1909. Pioneer Meat Market owner Louis Cassou (above, at left) and John C. Dickson, Escondido's "Raisin King," show grapes encapsulated in a huge ice block created at Cassou's new refrigeration plant. The population of the city and surrounding territory had grown to 3,000. Three schools, eight churches, and two new hotels had been built, and a Carnegie library was planned. A $20,000 sewer system was installed. Escondido drivers (below) are ready to show improvements to guests. Escondido was the trading and shipping center for a 20-mile radius. Railways exported 400 carloads of citrus and 500 of table grapes, although most of the grape crop went for raisins and juice. (Courtesy EHC.)

The 1910 Grape Day button (right) featured green grapes and purple lettering on a cream background. The design was also incorporated into the letterhead of the executive committee stationery. The county fair did not conflict, being held two weeks later; but the festival stretched the community's finances and time. W. E. Alexander served as president for the first of four terms. A depot scene (below) shows some of the 5,000 visitors flocking to Escondido on Admission Day and indicates the extensive replacement of horse-drawn rigs by automobiles. This year, festivities were relocated to the vacant Lime Street school grounds; the deteriorating building had been demolished earlier. Workers built a ramada and benches under the trees. (Right, courtesy PR; below, courtesy EHC.)

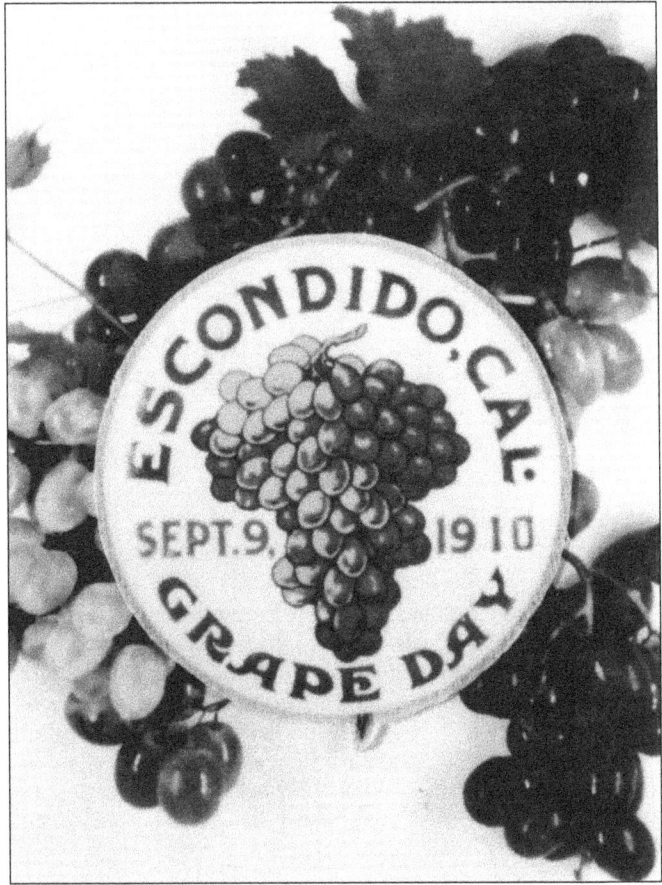

ESCONDIDO, CAL.
SEPT. 9, 1910
GRAPE DAY

GRAPE DAY
Escondido, Cal.
Passmore #1

Men flocked to join fraternal orders during this time. Membership gave a sense of belonging to a migrating citizenry, especially those uprooting their families to the West. Lodges offered camaraderie, common interests, and self-improvement. Many adopted inspiring apparel and secret ceremonies. Intricate drills and presentations were shared with the public at parades and gatherings. Most of the groups offered a women's auxiliary, usually with uniforms as well. Maccabee Tent No. 11 (above) members pose in their unique attire near Broadway after marching in the 1911 parade. The drum is marked Escondido Coronet Band, indicating a brother with dual membership. In 1910, the Knights of Pythias (below) are dressed in ceremonial garb of a totally different style. (Above, courtesy EHC; below, courtesy PR.)

Automobiles became so numerous that the parade committee created a special section for participating motorcars. This entry (above) is W. L. Ramey's 1910 Winton Six with Dean Howell at the right-hand steering wheel. Pepper boughs, bunting, and flowers decorate the car. Florence Ramey, daughter of the owner, occupies the front passenger seat. She later married Howell. Shaded by a parasol, Gretchen Huffman and Eleanor Williams relax on the backseat. In best bib and tucker, Grand Avenue (below) thrives on the crowd: stores remained open and the four hotels served midday meals. Church ladies continued their fund-raiser, serving a meal for 35¢ and ice cream for a dime. (Courtesy PR.)

A 1915 chamber of commerce brochure included this c. 1912 image. The panoramic view of Escondido valley from the west shows the presence of the mountains and the growth that had taken place in the city since 1896. Houses, commercial buildings, and industrial structures have increasingly spread across the valley floor. Grand Avenue, left to right just above center, is lined with buildings. Many are newly constructed of reinforced concrete, filling gaps between the

Displays were relocated to a ramada near the peppertrees along North Lime Street. Ice blocks packed beneath a long, shaded table kept the free grapes chilled until serving time. Refrigeration retired the grape wagon. Entering agricultural displays, young J. Paul Hatch won first place ($1) for his lima beans; largest watermelon ($1); and second ($2.50) on largest display of vegetables. The new, expansive location met with everyone's approval. (Courtesy EHC.)

prized Escondido brick business blocks and replacing many early wooden stores. The depot, packinghouses, wineries, lumberyard, and feed silos are clustered near the railroad tracks at left. A residential area spreads out south of Grand Avenue, with homes shaded by nearly grown trees. The imposing brick seminary that became Escondido High School towers above the community. (Courtesy PR.)

GRAPE DAY AND CIVIC BODIES

ESCONDIDO has two pre-eminent bodies that work for the betterment of the town and valley and show the live, enterprising spirit of its citizens. These bodies are the Grape Day Association and the Chamber of Commerce. The former association annually holds a celebration of the harvest of the vine on September 9, and at that time gives away many tons of delicious muscatel grapes and entertains its guests with an all-day program. In years past as high as 8,000 visitors have been in Escondido on Grape Day, and the day has become a statewide celebration, ranking with Fresno's "Raisin Day" and Pasadena's "Festival of Roses."

The Chamber of Commerce today has 138 active members.

Chamber of Commerce

The page devoted to Grape Day shows the chamber office. The group supported annual Grape Days as a way to showcase the marvels of an up-to-date downtown and the riches of the valley. In 1910, the city band disagreed with the conservative directors over festival payment but performed as a compliment to the citizens, playing not in the park but at a stand on Grand Avenue. (Courtesy PR.)

W. E. Alexander (left) exemplified the man of action. He arrived in Escondido in 1909, liked what he saw, and bought it. He purchased the 2,000-acre McCoy ranch, southwest of downtown, which he branded Homeland Acres. When the land was planted in muscat grapes, the 10-acre parcels sold well through his Escondido Valley Land and Planting Company. One cluster of grapes (below) measured 18 inches and weighed 8 pounds. Alexander featured the photograph in a 1911 booklet promoting his properties. He was dubbed "Booster-in-Chief" for his spirited and creative activities on behalf of the city and guided the Grape Day Festival four times as president. In 1911, Alexander bought the Escondido Land and Town Company and its remaining 7,000 acres. He departed Escondido in 1916. (Courtesy PR.)

The first shipment of muscat grapes in 1911 left Escondido for Los Angeles in early August. George F. Johnston, of Etiwanda, contracted for three years the entire crop from the 130-acre John J. Johnston Jr. Vineyard, formerly known as the Big Vineyard (above). The two Johnston men are not related. The fruit was picked by Italian and Japanese laborers from the Los Angeles area. Installation of concrete pipe (right) to replace cement-lined ditches improved the irrigation system. The view shows sections being winched into place for the downpipe to the valley near Eureka Ranch. The new system would force the water to surge up hillsides for additional planting. The Johnston Vineyard and central Escondido are in the distance. (Courtesy PR.)

Grape Day 1911 vied for attention with the final day of the county fair but succeeded in attracting an estimated 6,000 people, giving out 3,000 colorful buttons, and distributing tons of free grapes. A horse-riding group (above), featuring two charming children astride decorated ponies, pleases the parade viewers. One rider carries a banner promoting the county fair. The Grand Avenue scene (below) captures recent growth in the downtown, including the new two-story commercial hotels on each side of the street. The hotels served hundreds of meals but could not put up the multitude who wished to stay the Saturday night. Residents opened their homes to the overflow. Famed singer Ellen Beach Yaw performed for 650 fans that evening. (Above, courtesy EHC; below, courtesy PR.)

W.H. Baldridge, Treas.   J.H. Heath   Dr. J.V. Larsalere   J.W. Hedges.

Sig Steiner.   W.E. Alexander Pres.   Dr. E.B. Buell

W.C. Anschuets. Sec.   G.W. Wisdom   W.L. Ramey

Officers And Directors
of
The Escondido Grape Day Association 1911.

copy By

City voters approved incorporation of a Grape Day Association in July 1911. They also determined the event would continue to be held at the former school grounds with plenty of shade, city water, and other conveniences. The date for the celebration of the grape was fixed at September 9 annually. The purpose of a permanent board was to allow year-round work on the festival, rather than the last-minute hassle of the past. The board members were W. E. Alexander, president; W. C. Anshutz, secretary; W. H. Baldridge, treasurer; W. L. Ramey; Sig Steiner; G. W. Wisdom; W. N. Bradbury; E. B. Buell; J. W. Hedges; and J. V. Larzalere. Guided by Alexander, committees made big plans. Automobile trucks were hired from San Diego to shuttle visitors and provide tours of the valley during the day. Permanent improvements were made to the event grounds. (Courtesy PR.)

An endurance motorcycle race, starting from E. E. Wood's bicycle and motorcycle shop on newly paved Grand Avenue, was a highlight of the 1912 festival. The 50-mile course looped through San Pasqual Valley and back four times. Elmer Webb won at speeds up to 20 miles per hour. Bicycle, foot, and three-legged races were held as well. (Courtesy PR.)

Some of the crowd of 7,000 waits patiently for the free grape table to open. In 1912, a seminal year for the event, permission was granted to the association to use the park for all Grape Day Festivals, providing improvements be permanent and grounds maintained. Grand Avenue was macadamized, and Percy Evans began a daily edition of the *Times-Advocate*. (Courtesy EHC.)

44

At Lockett's Rock Springs ranch, the Escondido Coronet Band (above) played double duty when the county fair and Grape Day were held at the same time. The final fair in Escondido was in 1912. Grape Day crowds streamed in from Orange and Riverside counties; some estimated the visitors at 10,000. Extra buses provided tours to Howell Heights's panoramic view. An attractive dessert and ice-cream stand in the park (below) attracts customers including DonDella Ware (in white) and son Clarence (in white shirt and knickers). Nearby in a palm frond-covered ramada, 20 feet wide and 100 feet long, the churchwomen served chicken dinners and pies. Fraternal lodges operated booths and provided meals and rest areas for visiting members. With so many exhibits, contests, and attractions, no formal parade was scheduled. (Courtesy PR.)

Every able body pitched into Grape Day preparations. Chores included weeding (above), planting, sweeping, decorating, and—especially for the churchwomen—cooking hundreds of chickens and boiling thousands of eggs. When the call for help went out, Escondido High School freshman boys (below) were recruited from class to rush to the vineyards to pick the ripening fruit The boys enjoyed the break from class and, even more, the payment. The photograph was reproduced in the 1913 *Gong*, the school yearbook. All sorts of grapes besides the huge greenish-white muscat thrived in the valley. The *Times-Advocate* recommended to grape lovers: "hardy little wine-colored globes and big reddish-brown grapes with thick skin that suggests caramel cake and pear juice, or select small, emerald grapes with the tartness of gooseberries and more nutritional. There are plump lusty grapes too with a rich tang." (Courtesy PR.)

Margaret Juny (right), daughter of the rector of Trinity Episcopal Church, became the first Grape Day Queen when crowned in 1913 by W. E. Alexander. The royal coach (above) was the decorated Palomar Mountain stage. Queen Margaret's court consisted of Louise Handley, Jessie Carpenter, Gretchen Huffman, Carmen Conway, Gaile Wisdom, and Nellie Stiles. Harriet Larzalere was crown bearer. Brothers Dryden and Donald Beers served as pages. Eight young girls carried flowers and fruit in the royal procession. Friendly voting chose the winner, and a penny to the Grape Day fund earned a vote. The royal court, plus other young people, formed a chorus that toured the backcountry towns promoting the festival—an example of Alexander's advertising creativity. Over 7,000 people attended the festivities. (Above, courtesy PR; right, courtesy EHC.)

47

The park's new bandstand (above) provided a focal point. Grape Day 1913 featured games and sporting events. Headliners were "real Indian" men from Mesa Grande who danced in paint and feathers, accompanied by singing and drumming "squaws." A baseball game pitted the San Diego Chamber of Commerce against the local group. Dr. J. V. Larzalere skillfully sewed up a torn baseball so the game could continue. Instead of a parade, motorcycle and pushcart races occupied Grand Avenue. Ten big trucks brought from San Diego gave visitors one-hour tours. The fun seekers who flocked to the Hidden Valley left a lot of litter. Armed with shovels, rakes, and brooms, the Grape Day Cleanup Committee (below) poses proudly for a commemorative portrait with a vestige of the local produce display in a place of honor (left foreground). (Courtesy PR.)

Veritable fashion plates of the time, Escondido family the Mulkins arrives at Grape Day Park in Sunday-best attire to enjoy a 1914 event that almost did not happen. Some wanted to skip this festival in order to raise more funds and energy for a three- or four-day event the next year, coinciding with San Diego's 1915 Panama-California Exposition. They lost to traditionalists, who felt that once dropped, the event would not be resumed. An abundance of free newspaper coverage generated by the festival was also too valuable to pass up. Percy Evans, *Times-Advocate* publisher, assumed presidency of the event; and a simplified program was planned. Entertainment included band music, vocal solos, and the song "I Love You California," followed by a poem titled "The Escondido Grape." A procession of four decorated cars, each winning a prize, was the only parade. The 8,000 attendees consumed 2,000 boxes of grapes and 4,000 buttons. (Courtesy PR.)

Grape Day 1915 proved to be a stellar event. Directors realized the hometown would be competing against attractions such as the exposition and special Admission Day program in San Diego. They put best feet forward, ordered 4,000 souvenir buttons (left), 3,000 cardboard gift boxes for grapes, and planned the first official Grape Day parade. Cash prizes encouraged local people to participate, with each entrant paying a nominal fee. Dignitaries rode in fancy automobiles, followed by the stirring East San Diego band. The Escondido Volunteer Fire Department showed off a new red Federal truck (below). Queen Marie Wisdom, only the second queen, was followed by the Escondido band. Decorated automobiles, equestrians, floats, children's division, and clowns enthralled 9,000 viewers along Grand Avenue. (Left, courtesy PR; below, courtesy EHC.)

At the start of the program, Queen Marie Wisdom (above) receives her guests in Grape Day Park surrounded by her court—runners-up Grace Carpenter, Margaret Juny, and Virginia Hogsett—plus charming children. Marie, daughter of chamber president G. W. Wisdom, won the friendly "bought" election with a surge of 12,000 votes. Voting revenue paid for decorating the queen's float. Ellen Beach Yaw's famed voice thrilled the crowd with seven songs, including one that she composed about Escondido while en route to the city. Upon introduction to the audience, "Lark Ellen" was presented a beautiful basket of grapes by Rosemary Evans, three-year-old daughter of Grape Day board president Percy Evans. Little Irma Worthen (below) won a $1 prize for her portrayal of a jack-in-the-box in a cart pulled by Old General from Worthen's Dairy. (Above, courtesy PR; below, courtesy EHC.)

Decorated cars and horses were popular in this truly hometown parade. Many citizens participated in the spirit of civic support. A man and child on flower-wreathed horses (above) precede a four-mule team hauling a large wagon entry. The featured attraction, "California's Nightingale" Yaw, was introduced to this area by Escondido neighbor and Renaissance man Isaac Jenkinson Frazee. Yaw frequently visited the Frazee family at Woreland Park, its home near Bonsall. Frazee wrote, produced, and performed in *Kitshi-Manido* (below), the Pamoosa Peace Pipe Pageant, in 1915. The sylvan oak glen on his property formed a natural amphitheater. Main roles in this fable about Native Americans of the San Luis Rey Valley were performed almost exclusively by the Frazee family, with extras and chorus members from the surrounding area. The production drew huge crowds for three seasons. (Courtesy PR.)

The "Unkist Girls from the Sunkist Vale" (above) were hard to miss as they paraded around San Diego to encourage Panama-California Expositiongoers to visit Escondido on Grape Day. The unidentified young ladies wore Panama hats for the occasion. Newspaperman James Heath initiated Grape Day promotion. W. E. Alexander took the promotions to a new height, sending delegations of attractive young people throughout the county to spark interest in the annual festival. Carrying the Alexander stamp, methods were effective, drawing thousands of visitors to view the vale for at least one September day. The parade and program appealed to nearly everyone. To some, the delight of wandering in a vineyard, picking fresh grapes, and having the moment commemorated in a photograph (below) was a big attraction. (Courtesy PR.)

Local produce displays made a strong impression on visitors. Artistically arranged lemons (above) brought attention to this important crop. Homefolk and guests agreed that Grape Day 1916 offered a more rounded program than previous years. The parade gained participants; the audience was larger. Although no queen was selected, many surprises were in store for all. Sig Steiner received a gold medal honoring him as "Father of Grape Day." Steiner was a regular visitor and frequent speaker following his move to Los Angeles. Hearst International News and Film Service sent people to cover the festivities. Attendance at the chilled-grape table (below) and park attractions made good visual material for moving picture houses across the country. James Heath learned that 50 million people saw the newsreel within three months. (Courtesy PR.)

Two biplanes from the U.S. Army Signal Corps flight school at North Island, San Diego, landed near the park (above). "For the first time an airship was seen resting on the fertile soil of the Sunkist Vale, and for the first time, thousands . . . saw a sight never before opened to their vision," crowed the *Times-Advocate*. Pilots gave an aerial demonstration before returning to base. Another surprise was a radio broadcasting station assembled by Frank Axe and friends on top of the chamber of commerce building. The boys received messages from the arriving army pilots, Mare Island, Point Argello, and a ship at sea. A parade was the big morning event. Nearby towns sent decorated automobiles, marching units, or product displays. Parade participant Rosemary Evans (below) rides G. W. Wisdom's pony, Ramona. (Above, courtesy PR; below, courtesy EHC.)

Guided by W. N. Bradbury for the second year, the 10th- annual Grape Day Festival in 1917 opened with a grand parade. Entries were plentiful, with more floats and marching units such as San Diego's Sons and Daughters of the Golden West. Eureka Ranch's Moreland truck (above) transports the Oceanside band, which later played concerts in the park. Musical solos, humorous readings, and acts by Tom Hurley, a retired minstrel artist, provided other entertainment. Mesa Grande Indians danced. Ten tons of chilled grapes were given away. The Red Cross profited by $160 from the sale of boxed grapes; thoughts were with American fighting men in Europe. Local produce displays (below) impressed visitors. A Wild West rodeo in the afternoon enthralled the crowd. (Courtesy PR.)

Four

PROMOTING THE PRODUCT

Escondido leaders created Grape Day Festivals to alert the world that the Sunkist Vale produced the sweetest table grapes on the planet. They wished to extend the hospitality of the community while demonstrating the benefits that might draw upstanding people to settle in the area. Eight individuals guided the festival through the next 10 years: Dr. Edgar S. Buell, 1918; Russell S. Cox, 1919 and 1920; Milton V. Wisdom, 1921; Dr. J. V. Larzalere, 1922; Dr. Niels Matzen, 1923; Ira E. Leck, 1924 and 1925; Dr. D. R. Coleman, 1926; and Ray R. Solemink, 1927. The constant hand of W. N. Bradbury took the helm in 1928 for two prosperous years and continued through the entire turbulent 1930s. The Grape Day name was kept for continuity, but the emphasis turned to demonstrating the expanding agricultural, commercial, and industrial possibilities of the valley. Escondido stood firmly as the hub of Inland North County. Crowds kept coming each Admission Day. Floats became more elaborate; queens, more frequent; participants, more numerous. Professional designers were hired some years. New attractions were created. Even the Great Depression did not interfere; free entertainment and grapes provided distraction to fun-starved citizens. Repeal of Prohibition brought a boost to spirits and a burst of floats from local wineries. The war in Europe and approaching American involvement put a focus on patriotic themes. Delmar Gray directed the 1940 and 1941 events. In 1942, World War II interrupted the 34-year run. Most of the old guard had passed, and younger movers and shakers rose. Photographer Antonio Ricca led the festival's successful 1947 return. A polio epidemic cancelled the 1948 program. Directed by Jack Skinner, a three-day festival in 1949 overextended resources and interest. In 1950, western horseback groups, organized by Robert Vawter, dominated festivities. The numerous events overtaxed the community. Often considered the "Last Grape Day," the festival left the board a $3,500 debt. After an eight-year lapse, one final attempt in 1959 fizzled. The goal was reached. The harvest was in. No one would replant.

The Grape Day Festivals of 1918 and 1919 continued a patriotic theme. The 46th Field Artillery Marine band and Balboa Park Naval Training Center Band provided music, and officers spoke of their experiences overseas. A chorus sang the popular "Are We on Our Way to France?" composed by Escondido's M. L. Howell. Over 11,500 visitors received 6.5 tons of grapes in less than two hours. By Grape Day 1920, Escondido's population totaled 1,789, according to the census. American Legion members (above) carry the flag broadside, nearly filling the avenue. Ladies in white (below) ride in a white automobile that leads a parade unit into North Lime Street around 1920. Processions now featured lines of new vehicles entered in the commercial division by various automobile dealers. (Above, courtesy PR; below, courtesy EHC.)

The East San Diego Brass Band, led by equestrians, provides lively music for the crowd along Grand Avenue (above) in 1920. Vehicles transporting visiting and local dignitaries follow the musicians. Railways no longer offered special excursions trains to Grape Days after automobiles became omnipresent. A large float representing a grape arbor (below) joins the Midsummer Carnival parade in San Diego in 1921 to promote the upcoming Escondido event. Grape Day board president Milton Wisdom, Darwin Ting, George Yost, R. E. McConnell, Fred Eastman, Percy Evans, Lester Wright, Dr. C. J. Ridley, and Fred Hall ride the float and pass out grapes in small bags that were imprinted with an invitation to the festival. Wisdom (third from right) leans forward enthusiastically. The man next to him carries a long megaphone for making vocal invitations. (Courtesy PR, © WWA.)

"Milk has no substitute" is a theme of the San Pasqual Valley dairymen's float (above) carrying an array of wholesome children, dressed in milk white and enjoying the liquid seemingly from the happy cow on board. After exhibiting their flying skills, three planes from Mercury Aviation Company, owned by motion picture producer Cecil B. DeMille, gave rides from a field near the park to those brave enough (below). Flights cost $10 for a 15-minute loop over the valley. Free rides were offered to any couples willing to get married in the air. There were no takers. The demonstration was "to educate public to the possibilities of airplane travel," according to a dispatch. The company contemplated starting air service between Los Angeles and San Diego in the future, with Escondido as a possible stop. (Courtesy PR.)

Equestrians made impressive entries in the parades. This group (above) consists of, from left to right, Vivian Cox, Allene Prior, Ethel Rand, Marjory Cox, Betty Bradbury, and Harriet Larzalere on her pony. After the parade, everyone flocked to the park for entertainment, especially enjoying selections by vaudevillian Tom Hurley, the Laguna Orchestra, and the all-female Escondido Ukulele Club. Strumming members were Hope Crenshaw, Gretchen Huffman, Louise Crenshaw, Ethel Rand, Alta Wisdom, Louise Carroll, Harriet Larzalere, and Gladys Thompson. The "old settlers" booth, initiated a few years earlier, had become a tradition, attracting many to reminisce. An afternoon rodeo thrilled the spectators. At the "free grapes" stand (below), Oscar Hall (left) and Glen Young passed out 20,000 pounds of chilled fruit. Street dancing highlighted the evening. (Above, courtesy PR; below, courtesy EHC.)

More neighboring communities entered floats and vehicles decorated to show off their specialties. In 1920, San Marcos sent a float, drawn by 10 horses, carrying a display of diverse products. Fallbrook entered a truck display, and Ramona provided a small model of a poultry plant. Carlsbad-by-the-Sea sent an automobile (above) festooned with flowers, leaves, and a great banner proclaiming, "Carlsbad peas never freeze." A multigenerational family delights in showing off the gift grape bunches (below). The well-dressed family members are, from left to right, Nellie May Wooden, Sarah Delphine Weston, Edward M. Wooden (holding grapes between his teeth), driver Frank M. Wooden, little John Wooden, Francis Wooden, Ed Wooden (in straw hat), and Mildred Wooden. Not Escondido residents, they journeyed in the open touring car. (Courtesy EHC.)

After the death of longtime companion Felicita, a San Pasqual Indian princess, Boley Morales (right) frequently sang ancient tribal songs for appreciative Grape Day audiences. He augmented his meager income accepting tips. From 1917 through the mid-1920s, the board arranged with the residents of nearby reservations to perform traditional dances and set up a village to demonstrate their ways of life. Pala Indians perform a Feather Dance (below) at the reservation. This dance and the eagle dance were among the crowd favorites. Men and women from Mesa Grande, Pala, Pauma, and Rincon groups chanted, beat drums, and danced in the ancient manner to the delight of the audiences at Grape Day Park. (Courtesy PR.)

Queen Hope Crenshaw was the first royal lady in five years, and only the third to serve. The American Legion took on the selection process, as well as the concessions and evening dance in 1921. Queen Hope invited the runners-up—Helen Day, Clara Wessels, and Violet Peterson—to share the float with her (left). Uniformed American Legion members accompanied the float, viewed by 15,000 spectators. The Floral Society float (below) presents a butterfly hovering above a bower of greens and flowers. The butterfly was portrayed by Rosemary Evans. More communities than ever—Bear Valley, Bonsall, Julian, Carlsbad, Del Mar, Encinitas, Fallbrook, Ramona, Oceanside, and San Diego—participated with floats promoting their local products. (Courtesy PR.)

The Valley Center float was the crowd favorite. Fred Cooper designed a bungalow filled with a beautiful display of farm products such as fruits, vegetables, and grain—all grown without irrigation. The display was pulled by the first light-pressure superheated steam tractor, made by the American Harvester company. Loaned by H. W. Beers's store in Escondido, the tractor created great interest while on view in 1921. (Courtesy PR.)

"Pretty maidens amid the luscious grapes in one of Escondido's big vineyards" reads the headline of the Grape Day Special Edition 1922. Photographed are, from left to right, (first row) Constance Turrentine, Barbara Wisdom, Rosemary Evans, and Margaret Ashley; (second row) Mina Frankenfield, Helen Dean, Margie Stiff, Louise Carroll, Ruth Buell, Leona Rolfes, and Harriet Larzalere. This image promoted upcoming Grape Day in newspapers. (Courtesy PR.)

The 1922 Escondido Mutual Water Company float (above) is decorated with fruits and flowers of the valley, all benefiting from the locally owned, non-profit cooperative's delivery of electricity and water to 13,000 acres and 650 farms. The American Legion handled the queen selection again, opening the contest countywide. Local Ruth Wessels won the most votes and a Ford coupe. Seamstress Audra Reed volunteered to make the white satin royal dress. The night before the parade, the power failed. The gown was finished by the light of four kerosene lamps. Unfortunately no photographs of Wessels, with or without the outfit or prize car, are available. With the "Number please" entry (below), unidentified employees flank a grape-festooned truck with a map of the nation, bringing attention to national telephone service. (Above, courtesy EHC; below, courtesy PR.)

For a Grape Day weight-guessing contest in 1922, one huge bunch of grapes (right) consists of nearly 300 actual bunches attached to wire over a wood frame. From left to right, Casmir Clausen, Rex Peet, and Henry Adrian escorted the 4-foot-long creation to the park. According to the newspaper, F. W. Schulte, a visiting former resident, guessed the exact weight, 168 pounds. The Grape Day Board, led by Dr. J. V. Larzalere, raised $650 for expenses through a community auction. The day provided four bands, a Marines versus Escondido baseball game, evening carnival, and the queen's ball to entertain an estimated 15,000 people. Ten tons of grapes were distributed from the ice table (below). (Courtesy PR.)

Movie Queen Agnes Ayres was Grape Day Queen in 1923. With courtly words, Maj. Gen. Joseph H. Pendleton, commander of the U.S. Marine Base at Coronado, placed the crown on the star's head, followed by a fanfare trumpeted by two pages (above), Rosemary Evans (left) and Eleanor Henderson. This day, Ayres was "Queen of the Vineyard," surrounded by her heralds, pages (Barbara Wisdom and Winifred Prentice), wood nymphs, and butterflies. Board president Dr. E. B. Buell presented the actress with a silver loving cup, a gift from the people of Escondido. Moving picture cameras recorded the event for viewing across the country. A homemade automobile (below), driver unidentified, stands out among the many vehicles in the parade. (Above, courtesy EHC; below, courtesy PR.)

A major poultry producing center, Ramona created a float in 1923 that demonstrated the town's prowess in raising children as well as fowl. A feathery Rhode Island Red "rooster" pulls a pony cart filled with huge wooden eggs and featuring another distinctive resident of Ramona, four-year-old Lucile Kunkler, costumed as a fairy (above). At judgings in San Diego and at the county fair, young Lucile had been deemed a "perfect child" physically. The Women's Christian Temperance Union (below) urges viewers to "Give Prohibition a Chance; the Liquor Traffic had its Day" and "Obey the Law; It Takes 2 to Make a Bootlegger." Wearing LTL headbands, youngsters do their duty as members of the Little Temperance League in the 1920s. (Above, courtesy EHC; below, courtesy PR.)

Grape Day 1924 dawned with an exhibition of aerial acrobatics and wing walking overhead, a thrilling demonstration repeated two more times during the day. The parade moved up Grand Avenue with Margaret Stiff as Miss Escondido in the basket, with little girls dressed as flowers on the float (above). Mayor John Offett places the crown on Queen Trine Museth, with Miss Escondido at her side (below). Distribution of free grapes, concerts, speeches, a baseball game, carnival, and two dances rounded out the day directed by Ira E. Leck, board president. Escondido claimed to be the fastest growing city in the county: valley population had risen to 6,000, while 2,500 people called the city home. Grapes remained the major crop, with citrus catching up in acres planted. (Courtesy PR.)

Jubilee Year, 1925, honored California's 75th anniversary of statehood. The Grape Day board aspired to celebrate September 9 as never before. Prosperity in the area allowed the event to expand into four days. More people could visit the valley. A height rise at Lake Wohlford Dam (formerly Bear Valley Dam) that increased water availability was a site visitors *had* to see. The board contracted with Silver Crescent Amusement Company to provide concessions and entertainment, while locals focused on invitations, publicity, decorations, program, exhibitions, and the parades. The first day was traditional Grape Day, with Violet Peterson Graves (left), as Queen Concordia, and her court reigning over the gala proceedings (above). An estimated 15,000 people enjoyed the parade (below) before overflowing the park, carnival, and other nearby activities. (Courtesy PR.)

The 1925 Encinitas Chamber of Commerce float (above) gives the appearance of a flower-surrounded beach, with sand and bathing beauties. Irene Rupe (Swoboda) proudly holds out the Encinitas banner, while, from left to right, Leona McKnight, little Fay Rupe, Dorothy Gigax, Lena Westbrook, and three unidentified bathers promote the joys of coastal life. The float was built on a truck belonging to Emmett Peugh, who owned the first trucking business in Encinitas. The inviting scene won first place among floats. The flower-smothered automobile (below) represents the Escondido Rotary club. A Yuma Indian band provided music for the parade as the city no longer had an official band, and surrounding communities participated only on a reciprocal basis. (Courtesy Swoboda, © WWA.)

Discovery of King Tutankhamen's tomb provided inspiration for the 1926 Grape Day royalty. Emily Hershey portrayed Queen of the Grape. Maids of Honor Phyllis Blake (left) and Mary Matthews flank the queen, all costumed in ancient Egyptian–style (right). Dr. Ben Sherman designed a float (below) similar to galleys used on the Nile in the time of the pharaohs. The craft was red with Egyptian-style designs in gold beneath a bright purple sail bearing a hieroglyphic motif. Local Native American youths—Valentine and Leonard Kolb, Frank Sterling, Frank Castro, Howard Morales, Marcus Also, Joe Calac, and Feliciano Quisquis—portray oarsmen. Roman emperor Ted Watterson, offering a platter of Escondido grapes, knelt at the queen's feet. Reports declared this the biggest and most beautiful parade ever seen on the streets of Escondido. (Right, courtesy PR; below, courtesy EHC.)

The 1926 parade, featuring four bands and seventy-five floats, welcomed 20,000 visitors. Neighboring San Marcos sent a roadster bearing a "We Have It" sign (above) as part of its entry. From left to right, Elmer Brown, Roy Brown, Milford Brown, Theodore Fulton, and Marvin Brown pose beforehand. Kiwanis Club guard of honor and the San Diego Sciots band (below) precede the royal float in the nearly 2-mile-long event. The Ku Klux Klan won second place in the club division with a white float containing a decorated cross and two young ladies in costume. Two horsemen wearing robes of the order accompanied on white-sheeted animals. The Ramona float spelled out the town's name in brown eggs. (Above, courtesy EHC; below, courtesy PR.)

A novice 1927 Grape Day board, led by Ray Solemink, chose to hire a national special-events firm to handle the decorations, entertainment, and parade for a one-day festival, while the board and community groups took care of the agricultural and commercial exhibits. The silent film *Ben Hur*, starring Ramon Novarro, inspired the float carrying Queen Vanita Stiff and her court (above). The royal party's throne-like conveyance was drawn by a chariot and prancing horses. The re-formed Escondido band and several others set the marching pace. More commercial and industrial floats than ever rolled up the avenue before a crowd of 20,000. An afternoon performance of *Felicita* was advertised by a float carrying a tepee and costumed characters from the production. Queen Vanita (right) received a diamond ring. (Courtesy PR.)

Princess Felicita (left), daughter of Chief Pontho of In-ke-pah tribe of San Pasqual Valley, was photographed in 1915 for Elizabeth Judson Roberts's book, *Indian Stories of the South West*, a collection of tribal memories published in 1917. The tale fictionalizes the story of a Native American girl Roberts calls Felicita. The real Felicita lived in poverty and died in 1916 around age 100. (Courtesy EHC.)

With permission from Roberts, optometrist Benjamin Sherman wrote and produced *Felicita*, an outdoor pageant, which opened September 9 with a Grape Day matinee. He wove comedy and tragedy into a script portraying a Native American princess involved in nursing to health an American cavalryman wounded in the bloody 1846 Battle of San Pasqual. Professionals David Henderson and Mildred Voorhees perform the lead roles. (Courtesy EHC.)

Over 100 locals played roles as American Indians, Californios, and Americans in the Mexican-American War epic. Army officers and their ladies, on set in period costume (above), are portrayed by, from left to right, Howard Donaldson, Wilhelmina Bergander, T. V. Watterson Jr., Leona Rolfes, Alan McGrew, Ben Sherman, unidentified, Melville Howell, Joseph Espitalier, and Harold Peterson. Mexican music was an integral part of the show. Maximino Atilano (fourth from left) directed the musicians (below), all in authentic dress. Performances were held to overflow crowds. Famous people such as Will Rogers attended. The beautiful natural amphitheater was south of town. In 1929, the show was moved to another picturesque spot, now known as Felicita Park, and the production changed to June. (Courtesy PR.)

Benjamin Sherman opened his Escondido practice in 1924. He had a creative and theatrical bent and joined the local players club. Sherman was master of ceremonies at each performance and portrayed the male lead, Dick, in the 1928 production (left) with Voorhees as Felicita, the role she played in the hapless love story for five years. Chief Pontho (below), in inauthentic costume, talks with his daughter, Felicita. Local Native Americans had watched from the hills as Gen. Stephen Watts Kearny's dragoons and Andres Pico's Californios battled in the valley. The 1929 show gained more critical acclaim than Hemet's *Ramona*, started six years earlier. Productions of *Felicita* ran annually through 1931, halted by the Depression. Revivals were staged in the 1970s, 1980, and early 2000s, but without financial or attendance success. (Left, courtesy PR; below, courtesy EHC.)

Escondido Grape Day Festivals depended on citizens willing to participate in the production and work for the benefits. Two such people are Judge William N. Bradbury (right) and Grace Foncannon Brewer (below). Bradbury served on the first Grape Day committee and worked for the event throughout his life. He presided over the board in 1916 and 1917 and again from 1928 through 1939 and was presented a loving cup in appreciation in 1940. Bradbury ruled from the Escondido Municipal Court bench for many years. Grace Brewer and family moved to Escondido in the mid-1920s. Blessed with a beautiful and well-trained voice, she sang the traditional "I Love You California" during the program in the park from 1928 through 1938. (Courtesy PR.)

Few float designers had the creativity, skill, and passion that enabled Koerner Rombauer to craft outstanding entries that promoted the Hidden Valley and amused the viewers. He was a lumber trucker by trade, driving his rig to San Diego harbor to haul back loads for the local lumberyards. Rombauer was also an accomplished woodworker, making these tableaux in his home workshop. Using his truck and trailer for the 1937 float (above), entered by the lumberyards of Escondido, Rombauer depicted a farmyard with the housewife doing her laundry in a tub and feeding her chickens while the farmer feeds his pigs and cow. The *c.* 1934 float (below) represented the "3 B's: Buying, Building, and Being in Escondido," with detailed models showing three stages of house construction. (Courtesy KRT)

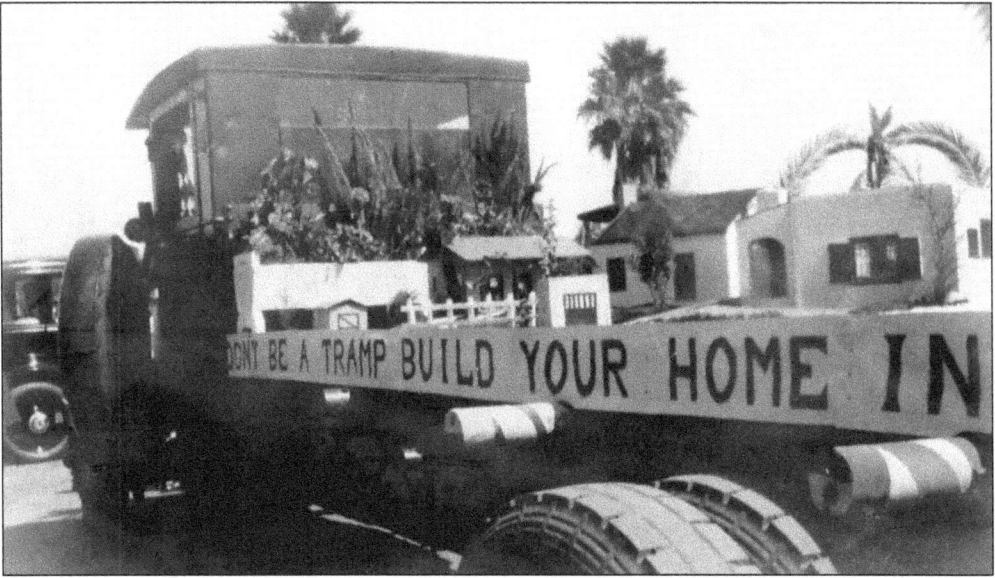

Another Koerner Rombauer float (above) was titled, "Don't be a Tramp, Build Your Home in Escondido." The model of a pretty town with comfortable houses of various styles was preceded by a homeless tramp on foot. The 1930 scene represents an established community, boosting Escondido and the lumber hauling business. The popular "Land of Plenty: Escondido" (below) entry showed the bounty of the valley overflowing from a giant cornucopia. Rombauer drove the rig backwards, in reverse gear, up the entire parade route so the crowd could see the beautiful part first. The 1933 photograph was taken in front of the Howell Feed Store with unidentified admiring women. (Courtesy KRT.)

By 1930, Escondido's population had doubled in 10 years to 3,415. The community enjoyed prosperity; citrus crops had expanded and brought good prices. Many improvements had been made, especially in the park. Lights were installed at the ball field, making night games possible. Exhibition buildings were relocated across the creek and improved, freeing up more space on the main grounds. The first public swimming pool was built, and a miniature golf course (above) was added. A huge crowd swelled the facilities, and the parade was declared best in years. An unidentified man and boy stand by a flag-decorated Case tractor entry (below) before the parade starts. (Courtesy EHC.)

Inspired by the popular *Amos and Andy* radio program, the Escondido Sciots club put together a comic parade entry in 1930. In the famous "Fresh Air Taxi" (above), Bob Lee and Stanley Trussell sit in the front impersonating Amos and Andy, while passengers "Ruby Taylor" (Charles Judson) and "Madame Queen" (Jack Denning) enjoy the ride. Gardeners and spectators considered the flower show (below) an annual highlight. The many types of colorful flowering plants that grow in the Escondido sun and soil made judging the prizewinners challenging. Noted San Diego horticulturist Kate Sessions judged the flower show in 1928. (Courtesy EHC)

GRAPE DAY SEPT—9-31 ESCONDIDO-CAL

Children dressed as flowers fill the 1931 float of the American Legion Auxiliary (above). The truck is wrapped in peppertree boughs and palm fronds. In caps and white uniforms of their order, members move into formation behind the float. The crowd enjoying the Grape Day festivities was reported to be 25,000 people. A pretty little Chevrolet roadster (below) is covered with sheets of newsprint promoting the subscription contest of the weekly *Escondido News*. The automobile is the prize. The *Escondido News* lasted only two years in competition with the *Daily Times-Advocate* and its weekly offering. (Courtesy EHC.)

GRAPE DAY SEPT 9TH ESCONDIDO CAL.

Freshwater and ocean fishing, as well as hunting deer and dove, were popular pastimes and food producers in the region. A Pabco paint truck pulled a gazebo filled with hunting trophies and equipment from the Cooper Hardware store during the 1932 parade (above). This was the silver anniversary of the Grape Day Festival, and Sig Steiner, G. W. Wisdom, and Judge Bradbury were introduced as the only living members of the 1908 board. The San Diego Sciot club offered a comical hospital scene (below) with doctors and nurses using butcher knives and blacksmithing equipment to operate on a patient. (Courtesy EHC.)

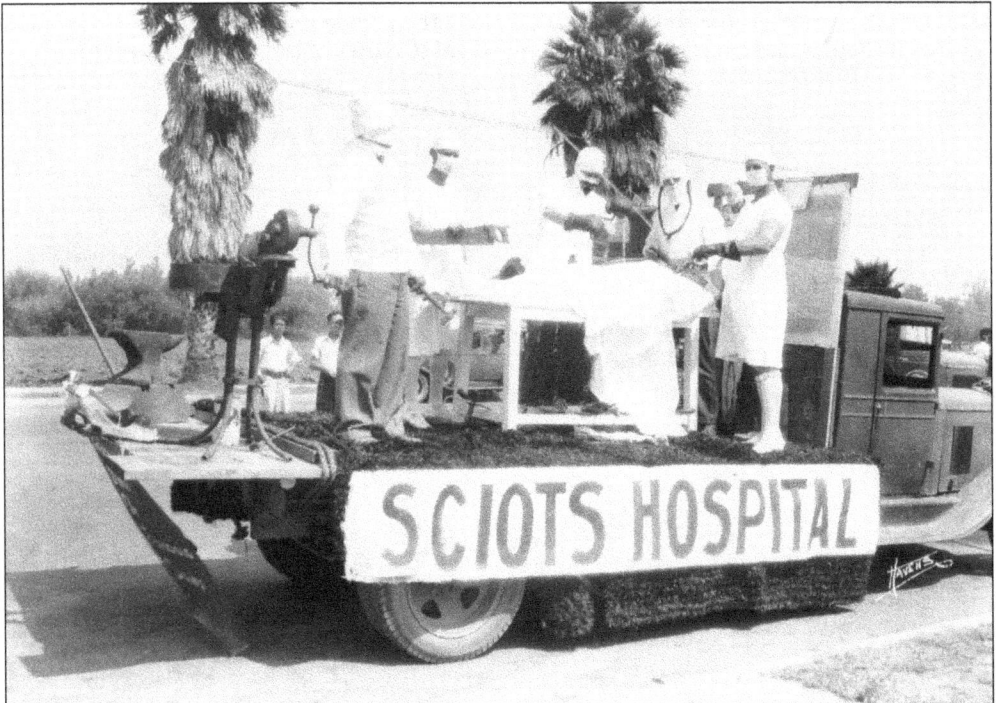

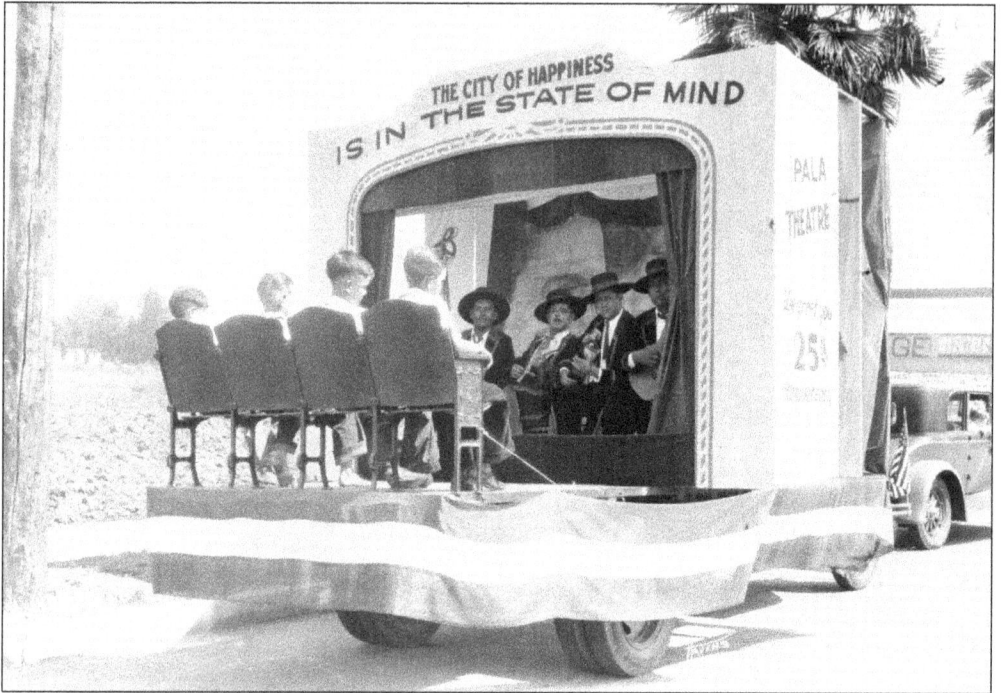

"The city of happiness is in the state of mind," proclaims the proscenium of the Pala Theatre entry (above). On stage, Max Atilano and his orchestra play to a full house, and Mexican horsemen in costume accompany the float. Film actor Billy Bevan advised E. H. Silcocks, manager of the theater, on the presentation. Silcocks was chairman of the 1932 parade committee. Pretty young women replicate the work of citrus plant workers in the Sunkist packinghouse float (below) while tossing fresh oranges to the throng of 20,000 along the parade route. Colorful Sunkist-brand advertising posters and crate labels decorate the float. (Courtesy EHC.)

Reported as the longest and most colorful local parade in history, the 1933 event drew a crowd estimated at 22,000 entertainment-starved visitors. Programs established to ease the Depression were featured in many entries. Postmaster George Bartley organized a unit that promoted the National Recovery Administration. Dressed as Uncle Sam, young son Kenneth Bartley (above) prepares to ride in an NRA-decorated roadster, which would lead marchers representing the figures on the NRA stamp—farmer, industrialist, businessman, and housewife. On the Humpty Dumpty store entry (below), from left to right, Mayor Andrew Andreasen stands with employees Joseph Green, Gary Duhurst (manager), and Keith Binford. The Humpty Dumpty logo is at the rear and an NRA eagle at the front of the flag-draped automobile. (Courtesy EHC)

While warlike rumblings were being heard from Europe, local Veterans of Foreign Wars presented a trio of floats in 1933 under a banner proclaiming, "Let Us Have Peace." "What Price Victory" (above) displays a mother mourning at the grave of her son killed in the First World War. Other scenes featured a trench and barbwire entanglement and a wounded soldier as "The Forgotten Man." The San Marcos chamber of commerce contributed a float (below) displaying a colorful mural that promotes the productive and pleasant land of its district. The super tall corn stalks indicate another bountiful San Marcos crop. The human adornments on the float are unidentified. (Courtesy EHC.)

Rosemary Evans (left) and Constance Johnston, as mounted pages carrying spears hung with *Times-Advocate* banners, followed Grand Marshal Russell Cox at the front of the 1933 parade. A sign behind the women (above) points the way to Hotel Charlotta. The American Legion band members dressed in sparkling white (below) pause along the parade route. The group, joined by some Oceanside Legionnaires, played for the crowd in the park as well as along the parade route. Band music was vital to the success of the day. Throughout the 1930s, L. F. Stoddard organized, taught, and directed numerous band and choral groups in Escondido. (Courtesy EHC.)

In the 1934 agricultural exhibition in the park, J. Paul Hatch won a silver fruit-dish trophy for a display of 96 varieties of vegetables (above). Born with a passion to garden, he first entered 27 types of vegetable in the Grape Day event as a 10-year-old boy. Hatch managed the Quiet Hills Farm of famous author Harold Bell Wright, southwest of Escondido. Wright chose the Hidden Valley for his retirement home. Hatch and Ramona, his wife, display a "green thumb" banner of ribbons (below) that she made of the awards garnered by his produce at local and county fairs from 1910 to 1950. (Courtesy PR.)

Little Bobbie Rayman of El Cajon (right) enjoys muscat grapes, just a few of the 10 tons distributed in three hours. The 1934 festival was outstanding for the 30,000 in attendance and the volume and quality of poultry and produce exhibits. Citrus displays were exceptionally impressive. The tangy fruit would soon outpace the luscious grape in production. Escondido now supported three citrus packinghouses. The program in the park featured the usual musical and theatrical entertainment and speeches. Rep. George Burnham (below), up for reelection, speaks of work in Washington and the future of the nation. (Courtesy PR.)

DAILY TIMES-ADVOCATE

Welcome, Visitors, to Escondido's 27th Annual Grape Day Celebration.

A Newspaper Promoting the Interests of Escondido and Northern San Diego County—the Land of Opportunity

Escondido Valley Is Truly a Marvelous Setting for a Perfect and Ideal Home.

Established 1912—Twenty-first Year GRAPE DAY, 1934 — ESCONDIDO, CALIFORNIA Volume XXII, Number 16

ESCONDIDO WELCOMES HER VISITORS

Every Person In the Valley Extends Greetings to All Southern California Folks

By ALAN McGREW

Escondido Ranch Products Return Over Three Millions; Crop Increase to Continue

By HARRY CRENSHAW

OFFICIAL GRAPE DAY PROGRAM

10:00 A. M.—Parade.

11:00—Giving Away of Free Grapes at the Park, under supervision of N. J. Nevin, assisted by Disabled War Veterans and Boy Scouts.

ON THE PLATFORM AT THE PARK

11:00 A. M.—Music by Escondido City Band.

11:15—Address of welcome, Judge W. N. Bradbury, President Grape Day board.

11:30—Song, "I Love You California", by Grace Foncannon Brewer; accompaniment by the City Band.

11:55—Address by Hon. George Burnham. Subject, "San Diego Harbor."

12:00—San Diego Y. M. C. A. Band; R. M. Forsythe, Director.

1:00 P. M.—Oceanside Elks drum and bugle corps; Mr. Tittens, director.

1:15 P. M.—Acrobatic Acts, furnished by the San Diego Y. M. C. A. Tumbling, Margaret Thompson, Robert Bridgman and Omer Stone; hand balancing, Har y Hammond, Ralph Stow and John Holmberg; hand stands, Ma ma Berlin; clown, Bill England.

1:45—Selections by Escondido Grape Day chorus; L. F. Stoddard, director.

2:00—Address by Col Ed Fletcher Subject, "Water Development."

2:30—"The Gingham Gals," from Oceanside; introducing xylophone, guitar, piano and vocal numbers.

2:45—Saxophone band in "toe-tickling tunes."

3:00—Accordion band from San Diego.

3:15—Address by Ed V. Izac. Subject, "The U. S. Navy."

—Talk, by Mrs. Elizabeth Roberts of Corning, Calif., authoress of "Stories of the Southwest." Subject, "Pioneer Days."

3:30—Escondido City Band; L. F. Stoddard, director.

4:15—Three-minute Speeches from different San Diego county towns: Fallbrook, George E. Kelay, Jr.; Chula Vista, Harry L. Olmstead; San Marcos, Mrs. G. M. Trent; San Diego, Elwood Bailey; Encinitas, Morris M. Myers; Carlsbad, Fred Mitchell. Other speakers to be announced.

4:45—San Diego Exposition male quartet.

5:00—Dance from San Marcos.

5:10—Japanese folk dance from San Marcos.

5:30—Trained seals from San Diego Zoo.

6:15—Max Atilano and his Mexican orchestra.

7:00—Encinitas Ranch Hands orchestra.

8:00—American Legion Band; Dan Oldham, director.

SPECIAL EVENTS

2:00 P. M.—Donkey Games at baseball grounds.

3:00—Baseball, Oceanside vs. Escondido.

7:30—Nightball game. Hoffmann's Pharmacy Girls' team of Escondido vs. National City Girls' nightball team.

9:00—Grape Day Benefit Dances at Big Stone and Veterans' Memorial Hall.

N. B.—During afternoon hours harmonica band sent by the San Diego Chamber of Commerce will play.

WITH OUR COMPLIMENTS
AN EDITORIAL

Percy Evans, publisher and editor of the *Daily Times-Advocate*, saw the need for and benefits of a special edition for the festival. Meant for home folk to mail out and visitors to take home, this issue was filled with facts, figures, and images of a progressive Escondido. Starting with four pages in 1917, and leaping to eight and then 12 most years, the printing increased to 20 pages in 1941, the final year of publication. Evans credited the merchants of the city with making the yearly promotion possible through their generous advertising support. For many years, the cover page design featured the same grape art and the schedule of activities for the day, as in the 1934 edition shown here. (Courtesy EHC)

Name *Charles Percy Evans*
Charles Percy Evans
Address 806 E. Fourth Ave.

Escondido, Calif Age 51

Height 5' 9"   Weight

Eyes Blue   Hair Gray

Occupation Editor

Employer Time Advocate
Chm.
     PUBLIC INFORMATION   R. Thumb

Two prime forces behind Grape Day were Percy Evans (above) and Russell Cox. Evans came to Escondido in July 1912 to purchase the struggling weekly *Times-Advocate*, which he soon expanded to a daily. Evans was a perceptive and progressive man, who thought and worked foremost for the betterment of the community. He also liked fun, joining the local theater group with his wife, Henrietta. Cox performed as first Grape Day grand marshal in 1908 and held the position leading the parade for most years through 1934. He sits on his thoroughbred, Chiquita, before a 1930s procession (right). A noted horse- and cattleman, Cox worked diligently to improve the livestock exhibitions and chaired the parade committee at times. (Courtesy PR.)

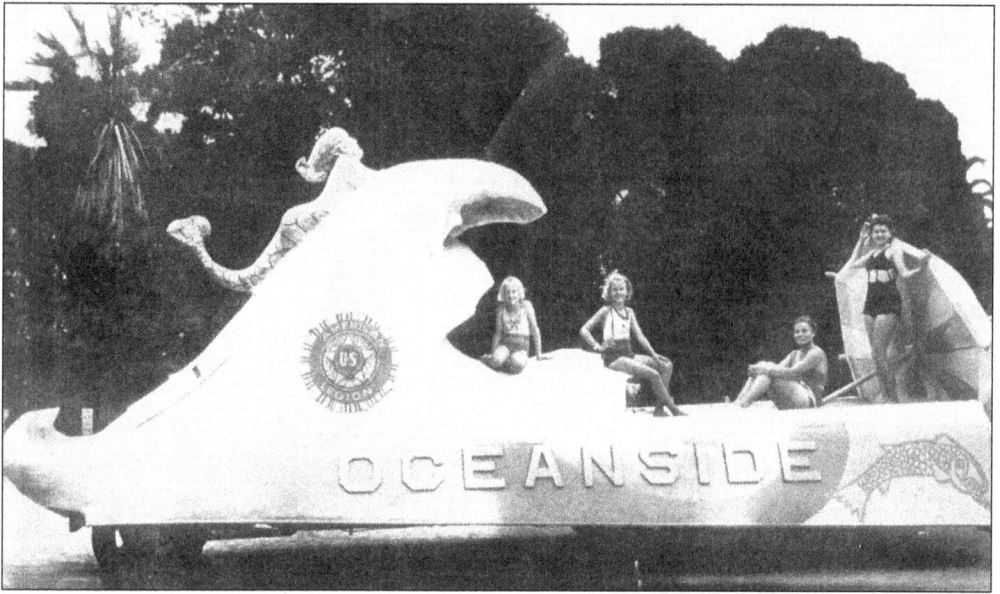

Surrounding communities sent a steady stream of floats to promote their home products, attributes, or events. Oceanside features a beach beyond compare. With ease of train travel, Escondidans considered Oceanside their bathing and cooling paradise. The 1936 entry from that city (above) features a wave-riding mermaid viewing an idyllic beach scene. The American Legion float carries, from left to right, Edith Rouse Swaim, Alyce Rouse Sims, Lorraine Fulton Shafer, and Patricia Tyson. A rare aerial view of Grape Day Park on festival day (below) shows many of the park improvements since the early 1930s. Many permanent structures have been installed and space improved by moving the agricultural exhibits to the west side of the creek bed (foreground). The photograph was taken before the adobe stage was built in 1936. (Above, courtesy Swaim Collection; below, courtesy author's collection.)

Publicity photographs featuring pretty females with grapes circulated in newspapers almost since Grape Day began. Two young women who participated in the celebration from when they were tiny children are Barbara Wisdom (left) and Rosemary Evans. They grew into roles from royal pages to princesses. The girlhood friends may be promoting the grape for the last time around 1935. (Courtesy © WWA.)

Around 1940, the unidentified beauties in bathing suits are not headed for the beach, but the Grape Day parade, to promote Ramona's Turkey Days on the poultry capital's float. Turkey Days boosted the backcountry and its fowl with parades and festivities in November just as Escondido promoted itself with grapes on Admission Day. Outfits created of turkey feathers became Ramona's fashion tradition. (Courtesy PR.)

With Prohibition ended, local wineries entered imaginative floats to display their now-legal products. In 1936, George Borra created a giant basket wrapped in vine leaves from a pickup truck (above). Two lovely ladies dressed in white gowns sat at the top beneath the handle, above the neat display of Borra Winery wares. The Palomar Riders (below) show off their horses and fancy tack along Grand Avenue. Stuart Hamblen and his Covered Wagon Jubilee, a 12-man group of musicians, performed for the crowd in the park. The famous Hollywood radio announcer and country singer served as grand marshal, riding a local horse. (Courtesy PR.)

The overflow crowd filled all the seating and enjoyed the cool of the shaded grass to listen to the program in 1936 (above). Grace Foncannon Brewer opened the program singing "I Love You California." The Federal Opera Company of San Diego presented *The Mikado* in full costume. L. F. Stoddard led a group of 44 musicians, contributing to one of the best festival entertainments ever. Dances and ballgames filled out the day. The beautiful Moorish-style stage (below) was completed in time for Grape Day. Victor Skinner, city supervisor, directed the Works Progress Administration construction. Local laborers made adobe bricks from creek mud and finished the structure with plaster. (Courtesy EHC.)

Boys riding decorated bicycles became a popular parade section. In 1937, Tommy Young (above, far right) poses proudly with his entry. Sharing the moment are, from left to right, brother Hugh, sister Norma, and dad Thomas. Numerous military veterans groups participated. In years past, several automobiles were needed to transport veterans of the Civil War. A lone vehicle carrying William T. Murphy, sole surviving member of the Grand Army of the Republic, was a poignant sight. The Epworth League chose a "We Want Peace" theme. The entry from Joy Dance Studio (below), operated by Joy Larrabee, features students dressed in white, tapping their steps. On the agricultural scene: citrus production had increased to 17 times greater than the grape yield. (Above, courtesy Young Collection; below, courtesy EHC.)

Supporters of the Ham and Eggs movement in California stand in front of the Escondido Headquarters in 1935 (above). Advocating "$30 a week for life," they admired the nationwide pension preaching of Dr. Francis E. Townsend. These pension schemes influenced the Social Security Act passed that year. Townsend, considered the father of the National Recovery Act, was the featured speaker at the 1938 Grape Day, talking on pension plans. The parade was rerouted to pass the new elementary school, high school auditorium-gymnasium, and adobe city hall. In brilliant red uniforms, silver cup–winning Merkeley's Musical Maids (below) stir the crowd in the Juniper Street area. (Above, courtesy PR; below, courtesy EHC.)

Rain fell on Grape Day 1939, the first time ever but not enough to dampen the enthusiasm of 25,000 spectators. The color guard (above) proudly strides up the avenue. The Townsend Clubs presented the common person's "kitchen band" float. The California Indian Rights Association float showed Native Americans in ancient costume and contemporary work and office attire, winning the cup in its division. Francis E. Townsend was principal speaker again, introduced by L. F. Stoddard, musician and local Townsend Club leader. His subject was "Let's eat ham and eggs and T-bone steaks." The Escondido Wheelmen (below), with their unicycles and semi-unicycles, are all dressed up with nowhere to go but the parade. (Above, courtesy PR; below, courtesy EHC.)

Although citrus production had become the valley's major industry, wineries entered the parade regularly in a show of community spirit and products. A reported 25,000 people ogled the imposing 1939 Pio Mighetto float (above) carrying a cask of wine supported by a giant mound of grapes. Four beautiful young women, dressed in filmy Roman costumes, posed gracefully holding above their heads the great silver trophy bowl that the winery won as first prize at the 1939 county fair. The women, two of whom are married to brothers Joe and Pete Mighetto, are the Meggett sisters. Volunteers (below) pass out some of the 10 tons of free grapes on newspaper sheets. (Courtesy PR.)

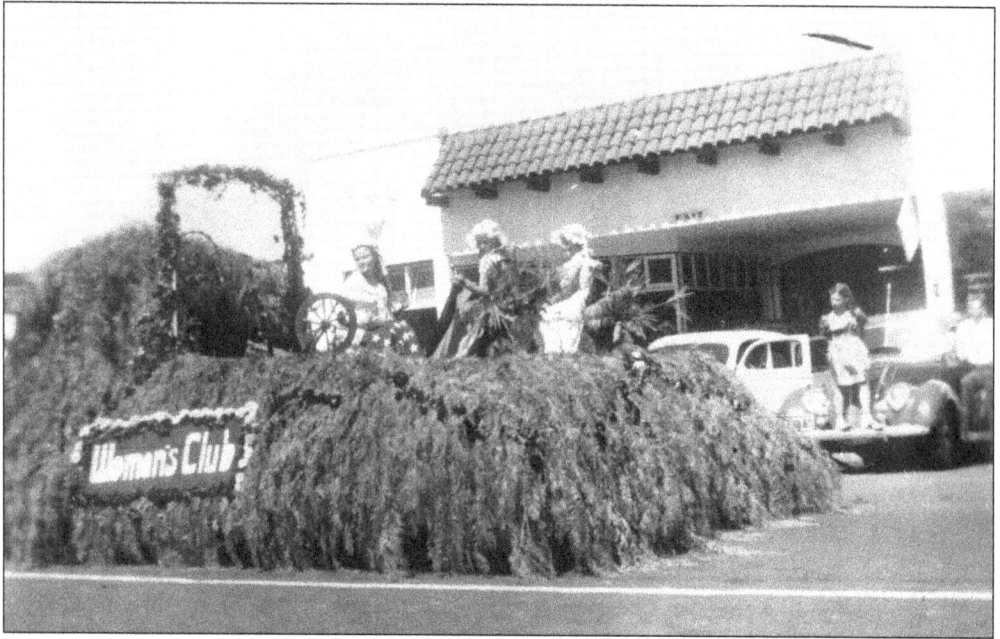

Westways magazine printed an illustrated article on Grape Day in September 1940. No Grape Day Queen had been selected in 12 years, but Mary Ann Willey reigned as queen of the parade. Patriotism ruled, too. The Woman's Club float (above) features Helen Millard portraying Betsy Ross sewing the first American flag, assisted by Sheana Wohlford and Romilya McGrew. The Mighetto Winery presents all its phases of the grape industry with a striking float (below) that also proclaims "Peace" and "God Bless America," spelled out in waxed grapes. As always, pretty maidens embellished the float. Luke's Golden State Service Station float carried 15 young men in comic costumes, performing stunts to make the crowd laugh. (Above, courtesy PR; below, courtesy EHC.)

An official Queen of Grape Day reigned again after a 13-year absence. Margaret "Mickey" Armstrong (below) was selected in 1941. The queen's float (above), designed by chamber of commerce secretary Pansey Claggett, was a cup winner, as were all Claggett displays. Queen Mickey and maids of honor Mary Frances Reese (left) and Anna Mae Agnew (right) rode the flower and greenery bedecked throne float in beautiful gowns. In three months, the United States would declare war on the Axis powers, joining World War II and making this Grape Day the last until 1947. (Courtesy EHC.)

Darlene Dyckman (left) was crowned 1947 queen. Escondido Bowling Center sponsored her candidacy, and she won by more than 11,000 votes. Queen Darlene and her court—Dottie Johnson, Bettie Butler, Holly Byrnes, and Nicky Bolin—wore pastel formals during the ball and on the float (below) and Western costumes during the two days of events. Children's Day offered a greased pole contest; sack, relay, and one-legged races; and bubble-gum blowing, grapes on a string, and a pie-eating contests. September 9 offered donkey baseball followed by a real baseball game. Street and Western dances capped the event. Photographer Antonio Ricca was Grape Day board president. (Courtesy PR.)

The "Postwar Grape Fiesta" parade, led by Jack Skinner up flag-lined Grand Avenue before 30,000 spectators, was one of the longest and most colorful. The San Marcos Grange float presents the seasons, with pretty girls dressed in white representing spring, summer, fall, and winter and samples of the region's year-round growing success. (Courtesy EHC.)

Uriah "Luke" Lucas shared Koerner Rombauer's super-creative float-building talent. Beginning in the early 1940s, Luke's Golden State Service entries were instant hits and long remembered. He performs as the barker on this entry depicting a classic sideshow with all the colorful characters hamming it up to the crowd's delight. (Courtesy PR.)

The 1947 parade looked like a duel of the privies. Heard Plumbing saluted the first Grape Day with an outhouse sporting a sign declaring it sold. "Chic Sales" is a common name for a privy based on skits about an outhouse-building carpenter created by beloved vaudevillian Charles "Chic" Sale. Fellow plumber Thomas Young created an amusing float featuring an outhouse and small shack where the "washer woman," with her dog, gets her laundry out on the clothesline. A U.S. Marine band played, and three contingents of Marines lined both sides of the route to Grape Day Park. The event honored veterans of all wars. (Courtesy EHC.)

A polio epidemic forced the cancellation of the 1948 Grape Day plans, but hope was high to host the event the next year. Proof enough is the 1949 traditional festival button (right). In cars donated by Peto Brothers Mercury dealership, 26 contestants for queen—from Oceanside, Ramona, Vista, and Encinitas—toured the north county towns to promote the three-day festival beginning September 9. Gloria Billigmeier of Valley Center (below) was crowned queen of the 41st annual festival by M. B. Young, while maid of honor Lois Hannaford and Mayor A. J. Kuehl (right) observe at a ball in the Arcade building. (Right, courtesy PR; below, courtesy EHC.)

Winning as best entry for community interest, the Escondido 20-30 Club float displayed varied agricultural crops of the valley, showing the changing emphasis from grapes to citrus, avocados, grains, and melons. Member William Barber rides in the center of the front seat with unidentified passengers. Grand Marshal Roscoe Hazard and Escondido police riders led the huge parade past 10,000 viewers. (Courtesy Fromm Collection.)

In the 1950 Grape Day parade, Lincoln School PTA promoted an upcoming Story Book Fair with a float carrying Mother Goose (Patsy Struck), the Three Little Pigs (Kenneth Herman, Susan Floyd, and Sue Ann Hovde), the Wolf (Peter Kuriloff), Wee Willie Winkle (Donna Shinn), Clown (Peter Winkler), Tin Soldier (Sharon Roemer), and Becky (Susan Johnson). The three-day fiesta proved to be the last official presentation. (Courtesy EHC.)

Tons of grapes from Highland Valley were given away at the park in 1949 as few vineyards remained in Escondido. Numerous changes had occurred: Freeway 395 had opened; Palomar Memorial Hospital was under construction; an A&P supermarket was on the way; the world's largest avocado packinghouse had been built; and $300,000 in elementary school bonds had been approved. Luke's Service Station float that year, featuring Snow White and the Seven Dwarfs (above), received first place in the business division. "Old Woman in a Shoe" (below) garnered Luke Lucas the best pageant award in 1950. (Courtesy EHC.)

Sporadic efforts toward future festivals fizzled. Beginning in 1954, an in-jest battle between North Broadway and East Ohio Avenue business leaders led to a "duel-of-the-grape-boxes" recognition, but not restoration, of Grape Day. A 1959 revival organized by Supervisor Dean Howell (left), who grew up participating in the celebration, featured a successful parade, served free grapes from Gasper Ferrara's vineyard, but also ushered out the Grape Era. Diminished agriculture, high costs, and changing times stifled interest in preparing, promoting, and attending the celebration. In 1955, Lewis Ryan put community sentiment into art (below) based on a notice Ohio Avenue businessmen ran, "In Memory of Grape Day," in the *Times-Advocate*, for the endpaper of Frances and Lewis Ryan's book *Escondido As It Was, 1900–1950*. (Courtesy PR.)

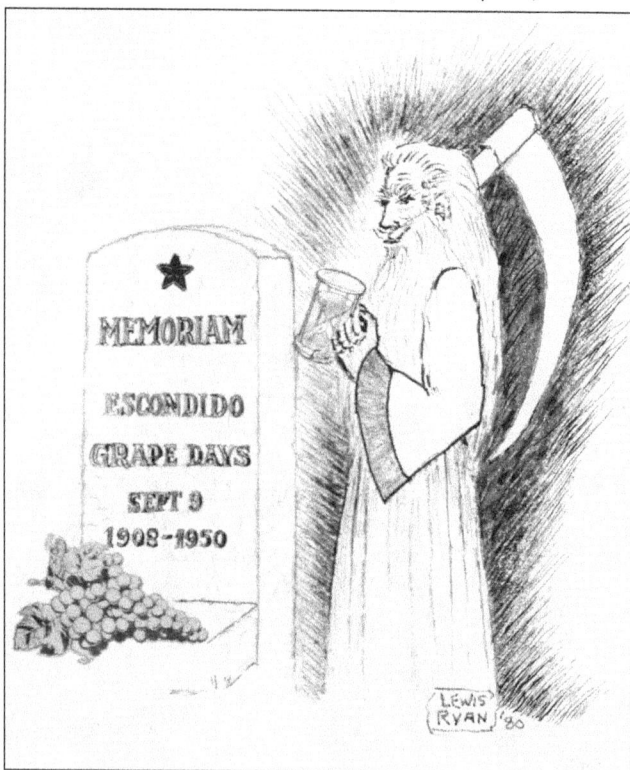

Five

ROTATING THE CROPS

In 1961, Andy Andreasen, Rube Nelson, and Luke Lucas toured Escondido in Nelson's Model T, passing out grapes in recognition of Grape Day, although the day had been retired. Only old-timers and *Times-Advocate* editorials publicly mourned. The 1908 goal had been reached: Escondido was known to the world. But the grape's place had been completely usurped by citrus, avocado, industrial, and housing production.

Recreational interests turned to Western themes. Horse enthusiasts formed Escondido Valley Riders, which sponsored public events over the years. Young men joined the Junior Chamber of Commerce (Jaycees) club for civic involvement and camaraderie. Escondido members decided in 1951 that a Christmastime parade would benefit local children. The event did help compensate for the absence of Grape Day. The Jaycees Christmas Parade has passed the 50-year mark, becoming a true Escondido tradition.

Other programs to promote the Hidden Vale have attracted crowds but lacked real staying power. The chamber of commerce created the Citracado Festival in May 1954, honoring the prime crops of that era—oranges, lemons, and avocados. Tours of fruit packinghouses were offered; free tastes of avocado spread and lemonade were served downtown. The multifaceted event involved nearly every business and civic group and many locations. The Jaycees ran a fair and carnival. Also featured were art and talent shows, Little League opening games, and an Old-Timers' Day at the park. Escondido Valley Riders paraded up Grand Avenue and held a two-day horse show. The festival provided something for everyone, but Citracado Days also faded away.

Kit Carson Days brought speeches and entertainment to dedicate the city's newest park in 1969. Pageant enthusiasts made attempts at reviving *Felicita*, but never captured the vitality of the original. A short-lived 1990 Avocado Festival introduced an unusual mascot. Escondido Historical Society, founded in 1956, offered guided tours in 1973 to honor Grape Days but turned to country fair and harvest themes for fall fund-raisers. Longtime residents still yearned for Grape Days.

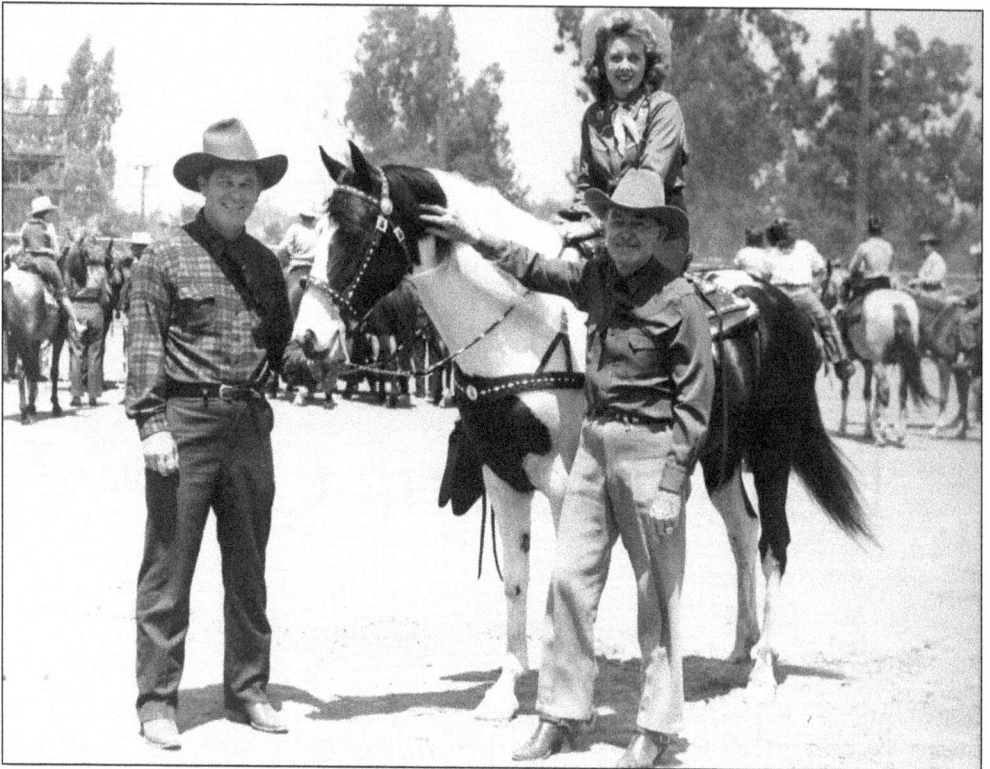

Escondido Valley Riders Association (EVR) promoted horse-related activities for many years in the Sunkist Vale and maintained a field and horse show grounds where Washington Park is now located. A 1949 event (above) attracted actors Gwinn "Big Boy" Williams (left), of Valley Center, and Harry Carry, of Pauma Valley, posing with Lois Niel (on horseback) in Grape Day Park after the parade. The EVR put on the Citracado Days parade and two-day horse show in 1955. A popular comical entry ambling along the Grand Avenue route (below) was a bull dressed in overalls and carrying masked riders. (Courtesy EHC.)

The mounted marshal and color guard led the Escondido Valley Riders parade along Grand Avenue in 1949. The group sponsored queens and dances as well as horse shows and rodeos. This photograph (above) shows off the beautiful mural of Palomar Observatory and the universe (left background) on the Ritz Theatre facade. The painting was lost in a fire the next year. Old-timer gatherings and picnics had become a tradition during Grape Days and continued long after. At the annual picnic held in Grape Day Park in 1962 (below) attendees pose for a keepsake. The tradition continues annually for 50-and-plus-year graduates of Escondido High School. (Courtesy EHC.)

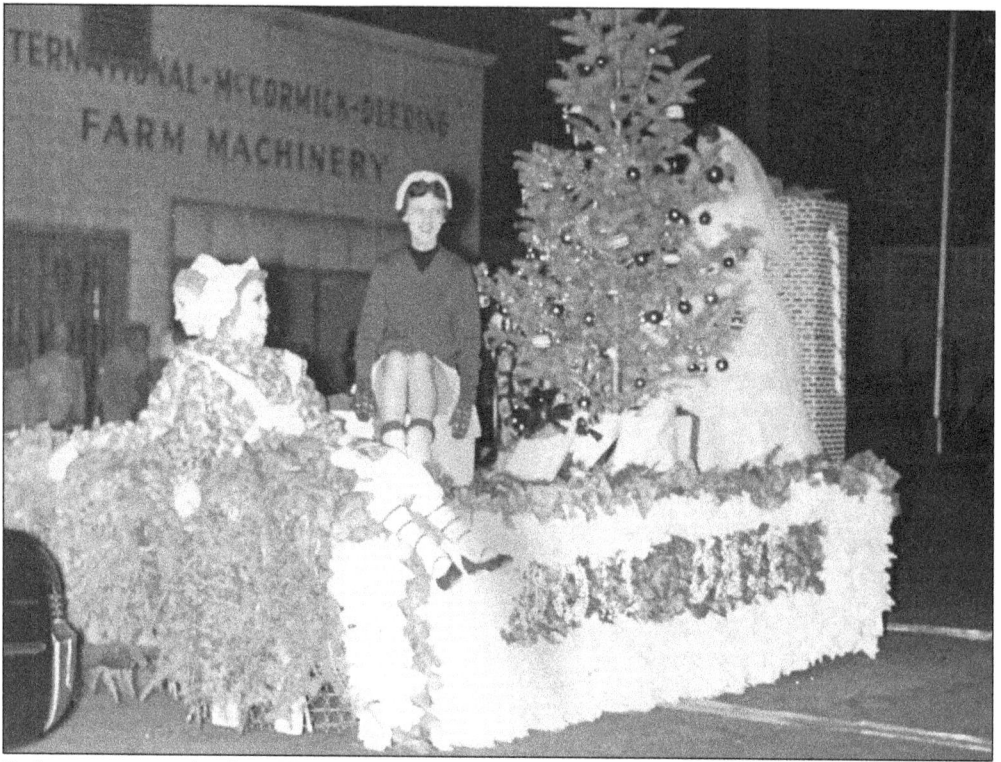

Before mounting the first Christmas parade in 1951, Escondido Jaycees raised money to hire 25 giant balloons from a New York City company already scheduled to perform in San Diego. The abundance of amply inflated characters thrilled the 25,000 viewers that December 3 evening along Grand Avenue. Following events were less elaborate, but the group persevered. The Doll Daze float (above) carries Lois Harvey, Beverly Park, Lottie Yoakum, and Oline Harp during the evening parade in 1954. The Ups 'N' Downs roller skating rink featured costumed club members (below) in 1959. Every parade ends with an enormous fire truck carrying Santa Claus to greet the children in Grape Day Park. (Courtesy EHC.)

For many years, a parade was not a parade in Escondido without one of Rube Nelson's antique farm or road vehicles. His steam-powered tractor (above) was a crowd favorite. The shrill whistle could be heard for blocks as the machine chugged along. In the 1970 parade, the tractor pulled a wagonload of people along the North Broadway route. The massive parade undertaking has survived chronic money and manpower woes but always comes off a rousing success. Only once did rain cancel the Christmas parade, and erroneously at that. The predicted storm dissipated, but too late to reverse the 2007 cancellation. The Fellowship House entry, always a prizewinner, spent the day glowering with disappointment (below) on its front lawn. (Above, courtesy EHC; below, courtesy O'Neal Collection.)

Kit Carson Days, sponsored by the chamber of commerce, celebrated the opening of Escondido's newest recreational area, Kit Carson Park, in 1969. The park is close to the Mule Hill section of San Pasqual Valley Battlefield, where American Dragoons, pinned down by Californio troops, were rescued with the help of Scout Kit Carson, thus the name. Mayor William S. Crow (above) speaks to the crowd during the dedication, surrounded by dignitaries on the dais. Queen "Kitty Carson" (unidentified) reigned with Colorado resident Kit Carson III (below), 86-year-old grandson of the famed frontiersman. The three-day festival included square and Western dancing, a horse show, talent contest, and barbecue. The event returned in September the following year for a final fling. (Courtesy EHC.)

Escondido Historical Society held fall festivals along Heritage Walk in Grape Day Park from the 1970s into the 1990s to give people a glimpse into household crafts and cultural activities from the early days. Grape Day was specifically honored in 1978. A local elementary school class demonstrates square dancing (above). Skills every pioneer woman should know to provide for family needs were also exhibited. In the barn (below), women practice yarn making, weaving, and quilting for visitors. Many old-time crafts are popular today as forms of artistic expression. The Junior Woman's Club sponsored bus tours of local historic landmarks, including a tasting at Ferrara's Winery. (Courtesy EHC.)

The society's first Grape Day lost money, so members opted for a country fair each fall, and finally a harvest festival. Entertainments and fund-raisers continued, but without recognition of Grape Days. Clogging, another historic American dance, became popular and of great interest to watch. In 1986, a local clogging group performs for the crowd (above). Mexican *folklorico* dances are always popular. A youthful group (below) demonstrates its skill in colorful costumes at the festival in 1989. The society continued the harvest–themed event with music, prizes, food, and fun until 1996. (Above, courtesy EHC; below, courtesy PR/NCT Collection.)

Escondido Fire Department members, made-up in clown faces to entertain the Grape Day Park crowd in 1989 with silly antics, pose with their famed 1926 La France fire truck, lovingly named "Old Betsy." Firemen restored the cherished vehicle and keep it on view for public enjoyment. (Courtesy EHC.)

The Escondido Avocado Festival of 1990 celebrated locally grown avocados. Gwynne Brack won the poster contest; Tammy Frazier, Robert Sawyer, and Sheila Barnett won recipe contests; but the tastiest morsel appears to be the fancily coifed, giant avocado mascot, being hugged (right) by an enamored toddler in the park. (Courtesy PR/NCT Collection.)

A small crowd ambles around the final harvest-style festival (above) at Grape Day Park in 1995. The event made a homey, happy place to spend a fall Saturday celebrating someone else's harvest and enjoying the other attractions. Already a historic transplanting had taken place in 1990, perhaps as important as the relocation of the historic buildings to the park to avoid demolition. A Tokay grape vine (below) was rescued from Mountain View Park at the direction of city parks director Donald Anderson. The last noble veteran of E. E. Chubb's c. 1890 seven-acre vineyard was replanted across town and thrives at the Ferrara Winery, a California Point of Historical Interest, as the lone living vestige of Escondido's memorable Grape Decades. (Above, courtesy EHC; below, courtesy PR/Field Collection.)

Six

REPLANTING THE GRAPE

Preparations for 1976 bicentennial activities rekindled interest in local history. The Vineyard, an eclectic shopping center newly built on a former vineyard, plucked the idea of celebrating the grape as a likely promotional event. For two years, it featured grape stomping, entertainers, and Lewis and Frances Ryan as "Mr. and Mrs. Early Escondido." Escondido Historical Society remembered Grape Days in 1978 but dropped the theme as unprofitable. In 1996, Norman Syler, EHS executive director, received notice that the society's event name violated a copyright held by Harvest Festival Incorporated. Syler and member Thomas Tuck simultaneously suggested reviving the Grape Day Festival name still registered in Sacramento. Grape Day reborn began with a procession up Grand Avenue to the delight of a small crowd. The event continued at Grape Day Park where free grapes, activities, and entertainment rounded off the successful event. After becoming director in 1998, Wendy Barker continues the festival with the assistance of dedicated staff, volunteers, and community support. Each year brings new participants. Grape Day Festival achieved the 100-year, though noncontinuous, mark in 2008. Modern Grape Day makes money, fills the park for a day, offers a nostalgic opportunity to meet old friends, and serves free grapes to every visitor while preserving Escondido's heritage. *Times-Advocate* columnist Robert Macdonald reminisced in 1976 of the arduous childhood trips he and his sister made with parents from San Diego to Escondido Grape Days. "We never dreamed that anyone actually 'thought up' Grape Day. I guess we just thought the Lord said, 'Let there be light, darkness, and Grape Day.' "

Grape Day Festival
and Procession

"Old Fashioned Family Fun"

Grape Day Procession -10 AM

Grand Avenue-Downtown Escondido

Grape Day Park Festival - 9 AM to 5 PM

Saturday, September 28, 1996

GEORGE FERRARA WINERY

Antiques • Art Exhibit • Contests • Prizes • Crafts • Equestrian Groups • Food
Great Grape Cookoff • Historic Re-enactors • Twirlers • Vintage Cars

Escondido Historical	Escondido Downtown
Society	Business Association
743-8207	745-8877

PRINTING AND DESIGN BY PRINTCRAFT • PREPRESS PRODUCTION BY ROBERT ABRAMSON

While sipping a glass of Ferrara wine and enjoying the vintage art on the bottle label, Norm Syler realized this image could become a striking poster for the society's Grape Day revival. The Ferrara family agreed the art could be used for event promotion for 10 years. September 28 was chosen as the date, and the Downtown Business Association became a partner. A traditional parade was planned along Grand Avenue, once the city and society agreed on the word "procession," as only the "official parade route" along North Broadway was allowed for parades. Former Grape Day Queens (1926, 1941, and 1949) retraced their route leading bands, horse groups, re-enactors, and antique vehicles. The festival continued in the park with grape stomping, craft displays, tours of relocated landmark buildings, a horseshoe tournament, political candidates, grape-recipe judging, and entertainers. Homemade baked goods for sale and free grapes topped off a good day. (Courtesy PR.)

122

The traditional vineyard art of grape stomping in a wooden vat was revived at the 1996 Grape Day. An unidentified woman (right) gives it her all, vigorously mashing the grapes into juice the old-fashioned way. An antique Fageol truck carries a mobile blacksmith shop (below) entered in the procession by the historical society. A blacksmith sits ready to demonstrate the equipment along the route. Grape Day Park is home to a blacksmith and wheelwright shop where Phillip Ewing teaches these crafts to students from throughout the West in the only such school in Southern California. (Courtesy EHC.)

The Orange Glen High School Patriots Band (above) sets the pace while proceeding up Grand Avenue in 1997. Juliane Gilligan reigned as queen, and the Ferrara family served as grand marshals. Mayor Pro Tem Lori Holt Pfeiler (below, wearing a hat) waves from one of the dignitary cars. Park events included crafters, food booths, live music, dancers, grape stomping, a petting zoo, pony rides, raffles, and the taste sensation—delicious grape pie artistically made by Marie Tuck. Queens were back to stay, sometimes joined by a king: Shekinah B. Barrett (1998), Edna Sahm (1999), and Karl and La Verne Stephens (2000). (Courtesy EHC.)

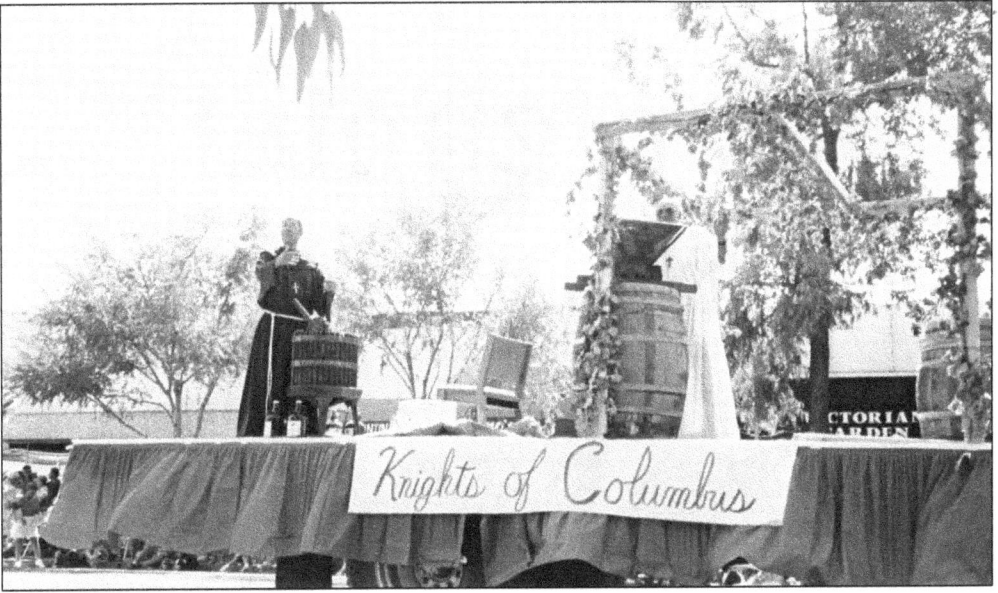

Knights of Columbus followed the vintage tradition with a float (above) carrying a padre stirring a vat of grape mash in preparation of new wine. Deer Park winery entered an antique truck (below) decorated with a giant bunch of grapes made from balloons, vines, and a wine press. Continuing the royal tradition over the years were Mary Bankhead (2001), Graham Humphrey Jr. (2002), Ruth Thomas and Helen Heller (2003), Thomas and Marty Tiedeman (2004), Doris Heard and Leo Calac (2005), William and Lorraine Boyce (2006), and Lucy and William Fark (2007). Replanted, Grape Day progresses into the new century. (Courtesy EHC.)

Centennial Celebration

1908

GRAPE DAY 2008

The sun rose bright on Saturday, September 6, 2008, to welcome the Grape Day Centennial Celebration about to begin with a parade up Grand Avenue, just as 100 years before when thousands of visitors arrived to enjoy the luscious Escondido grapes. On this day the festival celebrated the tradition of Grape Day, the vineyards having been paved over 50 years before. As the program (above) indicated, many traditions remained on the schedule—parade, reigning royalty, demonstrations, entertainment, contests, and activities in the park where, in 1905, the burdensome water bonds were given a solemn cremation. The Bandy Blacksmith business also was celebrating a centennial. Now housed in the park in a metal building similar to the original, Phil Ewing and the Bandy Blacksmith Guild perpetuate the craft. And, of course, the Centennial Celebration of Grape Day offered free grapes for all.

The 2008 Centennial Grape Day honorees have deep Escondido roots. Grand Marshal Allene Bandy Robinson (left) is daughter and granddaughter of prominent local blacksmiths Albert and Tom Bandy. She has volunteered many years to the History Center and encourages the blacksmithing program. George and Shirley Peet Cordry served as king and queen. Shirley's grandmother grew up in the San Pasqual Valley and graduated in the first class from Escondido High School. Four generations of Shirley's family are graduates of the local school. George, also an Escondido High graduate and avid supporter of Cougar athletic programs, became a founding member of the Cougar Athletic Club, working tirelessly to improve the sporting facilities. George is known for the printer's ink in his veins and kindness in his heart. He worked for 30 years, from sportswriter to managing editor, at the *Times-Advocate*. These three individuals represent Escondido heritage.

Visit us at
arcadiapublishing.com